MICHELLE D. CARNES

The Other Michelle:

My Two-Year Journey on the Historic Obama
Presidential Campaign as a
National Headquarters and
Presidential Transition Team Volunteer

LIFE TO LEGACY, LLC

The Other Michelle:
My Two-Year Journey on the Historic Obama Presidential Campaign as a National Headquarters and Presidential Transition Team Volunteer

By: Michelle D. Carnes

ISBN-10: 1939654289
ISBN-13: 978-1-939654-28-1

Printed in the United States

10 9 8 7 6 5 4 3 2 1

Library of Congress Control Number: 2014942287

Cover Design and interior layout by:
Legacy Designs Inc.

Published by:
Life To Legacy, LLC
P.O. Box 57
Blue Island, IL 60406
www.Life2Legacy.com

Contents

To my wonderfully supportive mother
and my great-nieces:
A'Jah, Eniya, Talise, Eden and Emeri.

PROLOGUE

One by one, she killed them. My best friend, Denise Snyder, was murdering another tune as she drove north on Interstate 75. The radio, a bit too loud, was losing the battle to drown out her off-key sing-along. Five hours into a twelve-hour drive from Atlanta to the South Side of Chicago. It was going to be a long trip.

My mother, Doris Levy, was sick, recovering from brain surgery and having bad reactions to anti-seizure medications. The most recent health diagnosis: Parkinson's disease. Sitting on the passenger side of my car, absently watching the passing foothills of the Tennessee mountains, I tried grabbing a slice of silence over the sounds inside the car and the noise of buzzing traffic on the interstate. I thought about what lay ahead for me. And about what I was leaving behind: two houses – one sprawling, the other a small rental; my sister Debra and her husband Dean Muhammad; her sons Alfonso and Eddie; their three precious daughters: A'Jah, Eniya and Talise; my friends from Chicago, Patricia Hart and Kevin Brooks; and a ton of other memories. After twelve years, I was leaving Atlanta and returning home to Chicago. No job lined up. No man on the hook. No idea of how far the partial drawdown of my 401(b) would take me.

Three things I did know for sure:

- I couldn't let my mother battle her illnesses alone, when clearly she needed her family's help, especially from one of her children, especially from her baby girl.
- I missed Chicago terribly, and had longed to return home for the past few years. I felt ready for semi-retirement. My age didn't dictate it. My body did. I was emotionally drained, after crying over my mother's health for many months. I was lonely and looking forward to a better future.
- For levity, for relief, and in part for civic duty, I'd decided no matter what else I did, I'd get involved in the presidential campaign of this relatively unknown former state senator from Chicago – Barack Obama.

What I didn't know was just how involved I'd become, and how invigorating that involvement would be. As it turned out, I became just one of a couple million Americans who joined in and volunteered for the Obama presidential campaign.[1] It was a historic time, an exhilarating time, a tense and frustrating time, an up-and-down time – and the longest two years I'd ever spent trying to turn belief, hope and a dream into reality.

So, why write a book? Why me? After all, I'm only one in two million.

Well, precisely because I am one in two million; because I had the great fortune of being vested in the campaign from its inception of the exploratory committee all the way through to the presidential transition team – which has given me an incredible ground-level insight into this historic campaign; because while other authors, including political pundits, strategists, analysts and news reporters, are telling their stories of the campaign from the top down or from the inner circle out, I can share the story of how one in this two million worked a job, helped care for a sick mother, discovered a new love, volunteered and traveled across the country at my own expense for this presidential campaign; because of my belief in the candidate himself and in understanding the power of one; because I am a student of political science, and this particular campaign was rife with teachable opportunities to engage the American public in something that I love dearly – politics and political activism; because my hope is that this book will also become a teaching tool to inspire subsequent generations to get engaged in our American political system; because within this story are two million little stories that are mine and yours alike, and in sharing mine, I am sharing yours, too; because my story is history that should be told – albeit personal history, it is history nonetheless; and lastly, because my three little great-nieces are

---

[1] As reported in a feature story on Chris Hughes, creator of the MyBarackObama website, by Erick Schonfeld in *TechCrunch* on March 17, 2009: "By the time the campaign was over, volunteers had created more than 2 million profiles on the site, planned 200,000 offline events, formed 35,000 groups, posted 400,000 blogs, and raised $30 million on 70,000 personal fund-raising pages."

too young to know or understand what was happening all around them during the 2007–2008 campaign season, so I'd like to provide them (and their generation) with a document that describes just how sacrificial it was for everyday working people to hit the pause buttons on our lives to campaign, and donate, and canvass, and vote for the first black president of the United States.

So, for all of these reasons, I've written this book. It is my profound hope that you will learn, laugh and enjoy the journey.

Michelle D. Carnes
January 2010

CHAPTER
One
NATIONAL CAMPAIGN
GETTING INTO THE CALL CENTER

From the moment I stepped off the eleventh floor elevators, every-thing felt right. Moving up the teal carpeted hall towards the massive glass doors stenciled with the now-famous Obama insignia, I knew I'd made the right decision: support the underdog – especially one with class.

The Obama for America (OFA) national headquarters was located in prime downtown Chicago territory, on South Water Street between Michigan Avenue and Lower Wacker Drive. It took up the entire eleventh floor of the mammoth black steel and glass structure that straddled both sides of South Water Street. At the time, its actual address was a secret. Only paid staff and trusted Secret-Service-vetted volunteers knew the exact location. That address was 223 North Michigan Avenue.

Wow! How can this puny campaign afford this gem? I asked myself.

I later learned that this small, flying-under-the-radar campaign was built, engineered and driven by some very shrewd, smart, smooth and frugal staffers. David Axelrod was chief among them. He'd been instru-mental in getting the prime office space at a fire-sale price, because the 33,000 square feet that the campaign leased from Accenture (formerly part of the Arthur Andersen accounting firm) had previously been empty.[2]

---

[2] In Lynn Sweet's "Obama's New HQ Has Room to Move," Chicago Sun-Times, April 6, 2007, [http://www.suntimes.com/news/sweet/330364.CST-NWS-sweet06.article], she reports, "the campaign took over a turn-key sublease from Accenture, 33,000 square feet complete with sleek blond custom workstations, meeting rooms and space for the various departments."

I was six minutes early for my 2:00 p.m. interview with the manager of the OFA Call Center. I checked in with an almost too perky college kid with shoulder length brown hair and a white cotton, button-down blouse.

"Welcome to Obama for America!" she chirped. "How may I help you!"

"I have a 2 o'clock appointment with Mr. Mason," I replied, showing her my date-stamped, clip-on visitor pass from the security guard in the downstairs lobby.

"Okay, Ms. Cranes. I see that we have your name here. I'll ring Mr. Mason, okay!"

"Um, it's Carnes."

"Pardon me, Ms. Cranes," she said, dialing the phone.

"It's *Carnes*. *Michelle Carnes*, his 2 o'clock appointment."

"Oh, sorry," giggled Ms.-Perky-College-Kid. "You're right – hey Mason, Ms. *Carnes*, your 2 o'clock is here."

After listening for a moment, perky-kid's face morphed into a little fist as she apparently heard news that she didn't want or expect to receive. "Okay, thanks. I'll tell her."

It turned out that Mr. Mason couldn't keep our meeting because he was heading to a managers' meeting. Perky-kid rattled off a list of maybes from which I could choose: maybe I could schedule again; maybe I could sit and read a magazine while waiting until the non-time-determined meeting was over; maybe I could talk to someone else, if I didn't mind waiting until she could locate someone.

My thought was *maybe I can just take my black self back home and give my free skills and services to another campaign*. My response, however, was, "I've been emailing Liz Utrup back and forth. She set up the meeting. Maybe I can talk her."

I sat on one of the cushiony, rust-colored, leather sofas, grabbed a magazine and absently flipped through the pages. I knew why I was relegated to the waiting room instead of sitting in Mr. Mason's office. I was an unknown. Not a "nobody," just an unknown. The game that Mr. Mason was playing was as old as Chicago politics itself. It appeared to him that I'd just appeared on the doorstep of this campaign without being properly recommended by/referred from/introduced by way of/ linked in/social networked/in-lawed/married to/or hooked-up to anybody. By some fluke, I just appeared. The truth was that I didn't just appear. I'd become involved with the Obama campaign when he was running for United States senator. Nearly three years earlier, on a visit home in September of 2004, I read in the *Chicago Tribune* that senatorial candidate Obama had opened a downtown office. The next day, I boarded the Metra Blue Island commuter train at 121st and State Street and rode it downtown to the Jackson-Van Buren stop. An hour later, I was showing my Georgia driver's license to the security guard in the lobby, filling in the "purpose of visit" column on the sign-in sheet with the words "campaign donation."

The security guard cleared me to go upstairs, where I was greeted by a kind smile from a woman with an African accent.

"Well-come. To the Obama for See-knit campaign," she said warmly. *"Do you have an appoint mint wit someone?"*

"No, ma'am," I said nervously, feeling a bit foolish. *"I-I'm just here ta make a donation."*

"Well, bless you, sista'. Here, come pleat this form first," she replied.

I completed the donor information form and handed it back to her with a check for one hundred dollars.

"My God, sista'. You have traveled all thee way from George-Gee-Ah? To give to the campaign? Thank you! Bless you!"

And that's how I initially got connected to the Obama campaign. Since that September day and $100 donation, I'd become part of their email database and mailing list. I'd since received tickets for the 2004 election night watch and victory party; an invitation in December 2006 to donate to the Obama for President exploratory committee, to which I gave $250; an invitation to join the Georgians for Obama online social network group, which I joined and participated in weekly phone-in planning meetings; and upon sending an email notice to the national campaign headquarters that I'd be moving back to Chicago, I'd received an email from Liz Utrup to join the Chicago campaign upon my return – which brought me to the brick wall I was facing now.

I'd decided that I wasn't going to run all of these facts down to Perky-kid, Mr. Mason, or anyone else. I wasn't going to hand in my resume, go through an interview, be checked out by the Secret Service to work for free for a campaign that appeared to be open and honest on the surface, but was the same ol' political bullcrap underneath. I simply decided to leave. And just as I did, Liz Utrup walked out.

"Hi, Ms. Carnes. I'm Liz Utrup," a tall, slender, girl-next-door-looking young lady said as she shook my hand. "I'm so sorry for the mix-up. We didn't keep you waiting too long, did we?"

"No, Ms. Utrup, you didn't," I responded with a smile and handshake.

"Oh, please call me Liz."

"Okay, Liz. Please call me Michelle."

"Well, Michelle. Welcome to the national headquarters of the Obama for America campaign!"

In that split-second exchange of warm greetings, I decided to put my apprehensions aside for the moment and just see how things would play out. After all, I'd heard this candidate's speech, read his book, *Audacity of Hope*, felt that I could believe in his message, and really did want to be a part of something that would be truly historic if he won the presidency. *Maybe this campaign really is genuine and on the up-and-up*, I thought. Maybe Mr. Mason is the real fluke. So I followed as Liz led me through a massive wooden door that opened into a massive wall-of-windows conference room, and on to her meager desk in a small room marked "Call Center."

THE LAYOUT OF THE NHQ

As it turned out, Mr. Mason was a fluke. He wasn't at all cut from the same cloth as the other Obama staffers and volunteers. He was a skinny, black kid who walked hunched-shouldered, no smile, carried a big stick. Like the majority of people at the national headquarters (NHQ), he was young and college-educated, except he was rude and witless. He was the manager of the Call Center, and Liz was the assistant manager. He'd speak to her, but not to the volunteers. He'd laugh and talk to other staffers, but not to us. He'd greet the white workers, but not fellow blacks. He'd ask staffers to do something. He'd tell us. About three weeks into my tenure at NHQ, he got fired.

Liz was immediately promoted to manager, and the whole tone of that office changed for the better. She was calm and courteous, pleasant to be around. She seemed to get that we were volunteers – meaning we worked for free – and were the lifeblood of the Call Center. Although nearly one hundred staff members worked at the NHQ, Liz and the intern were the only paid staff in the Call Center. And by the end of the campaign, over seven hundred volunteers were working at the NHQ, with the largest majority being in the Call Center.[3] Liz had to staff, manage and schedule an all-volunteer call center, which was a real juggling act. And when one of the balls dropped, she'd pick up the slack and cover the phones herself.

I volunteered twice a week, for four hours each day. Each time I met someone new – Kathy, a retired insurance adjuster; Isaac, president of a small technology and marketing company; Joyce, a retiree from Obama's state senate office; Dr. Cynthia Barnes, an adult education administrator who later became a good friend. I was meeting new people, learning the Call Center scripts, and learning more about candidate Obama's positions on war, terrorism, education, women's issues, reproductive rights, the economy, race and class, racial profiling, volunteering and giving back. I was enjoying all of this newness. It was refreshing and intoxicating. Some of those good vibes must have rubbed off on my mother as well. She no longer walked sideways. Her gait was loosening and strides becoming more normal. She seemed to take heart in our weekly trips to

---

[3] The number of paid staff at national headquarters, reported in an article by CBS 2 Political Editor Mike Flannery, titled "Obama Campaign Headquarters Buzzes With Excitement," April 5, 2007. The number of volunteer workers at the national headquarters is based on an internal thank you email sent to NHQ volunteers at the end of the campaign.

the University of Chicago Hospital for physical therapy for her legs and thighs, with me driving and her riding and looking out at the city from the car.

I quickly learned my way around the NHQ. Not an easy task, since the vast headquarters consisted of a series of octagon-shaped computer desks, clusters of offices in each corner, and endless departments and units focused on their own unique organizational function or demographic group:

- There was the *Finance Department*, the powerful fundraising arm of the campaign that brought the money in; not to be confused with the *Accounting Department*, which paid the money out, or confused with the *Operations Department*, which accepted incoming bills and invoices from catering, stage productions, marketing, real estate and various other companies from across the country, that had to be matched against files and files of contracts (created by the *Legal Department*) and okayed to be paid by the aforementioned Accounting Department.

- Then there was the *Mail Room*, which received all incoming mail, boxes, packages and correspondence of every imaginable texture, shape and size; not to be confused with the *Correspondence Department*, which responded to all general correspondence, both written and electronic, through its separate written and email correspondence teams.

- Then there was the *Media Department*, responsible for monitoring the media's coverage and accuracy of the candidate and his positions; not to be confused with the *New Media Department*, which managed and converted old media formats such as news clips, tapes and videos into new media formats such as YouTube videos, Flickr photos, and Facebook social network pages. And within the New Media Department lay the tiny yet powerful *Online Organizing* team headed by Chris Hughes, director of the enormous "my.barackobama.com" network groups' site, which was part of the behemoth "www.barackobama.com" website, managed by the Webmaster and *IT Department.*

• And then there were even more and more and more departments, from *Political,* which handled all things political – from interacting with local, state and national politicians to research to developing policy statements; to *Outreach,* which coordinated activities amongst the vast and growing specialty groups of supporters, from the "First Americans for Obama," to the "African Americans for Obama," to the "Asian Americans for Obama," to the Veterans for. . ., the Independents for. . ., and even "Republicans for Obama"; to *Research,* which provided opposition research on opposing candidates, not to be confused with the research provided by each department or unit, which cranked out their respective policy statements that the Call Center relayed to incoming callers.

One thing I readily noticed was that each time that I came and went, Liz was there. Always. If I came in at ten in the morning, or at two in the afternoon, or when I stayed late and left at eight in the evening, she was there. And surprisingly, her demeanor, tone and management style were always the same: calm, quiet, reassuring. This style, which permeated through many of Obama staffers and volunteers, became the campaign's hallmark descriptive phase: "no drama Obama." About a month into working, I noticed that not only was Liz always there, but a lot of the other young folks were always there too. They seemed to practically live at the NHQ. As it turned out, they practically were. There were three kitchens with refrigerators, microwaves and water purification machines; four bathrooms, including a unisex one; a nearby gym where many of the young staffers worked out, swam, steamed, showered; a ping-pong table for relaxing or releasing stress; and little by little more and more sofas and love seats donated by well-intended, well-off donors began occupying individual and open office spaces.

Not only were the young staffers "always" at the NHQ, but they relentlessly worked incredibly long hours – twelve, thirteen, fourteen hours a day. They were smart, tech-savvy, focused, and they were the bosses.

My best estimate of the ratio of young to old campaign staffers and volunteers was about 3 to 1. As reported, the median age was 22.[4] In fact, Liz, my boss, was in her early twenties, which made her young enough to be my child. And yet, I had absolutely no problem taking direction from her or respecting her leadership. Three things I learned early on in this campaign:

1. Utilizing the energy, technology skills, idealism, and passion of young people was one of the core strategies of this campaign. What I understood and saw early on, and what people on the outside of the NHQ did not, is that from the onset the Obama campaign had begun drafting young people as young as 18 years old to be active, grassroots, on-the-ground participants in the campaign. This fact was demonstrated to me back in February 2007 when I joined the Georgians for Obama social network group. One of the group participants was an 18-year-old high school senior named Danny. He was the precinct captain for his high school – yes, that's right, precinct captain. Can you imagine the power blast to the ego this title carries for a passionate, civic-minded young person? The process of becoming a precinct captain involved getting signed permission from the school principal to allow the young captain to coordinate voting registration drives at his school – his precinct. How smart was this move? Very smart, very shrewd, very quiet and low-key. Slowly and quietly this type of activity was happening across the country, unfolding like a yawning rainbow from "red state" Georgia to "purple" Colorado to the bluest of "blue states," California. And it was all happening ten months before the Iowa caucus! And well before other presidential candidates and the outside world even got wind of how important young people really were to the campaign.

---

[4] Eric Greenberg, author of Generation We and widely viewed as an expert on the behavior of the Millennial Generation, reported to Olivia Ward of *The Toronto Star*, in an article titled "Looking at How Obama Brought Youth to the Polls," November 10, 2008, the following: "In Obama's campaign, there were 5,000 paid field organizers with a median age of 22."

2. The second thing I learned early on was that these young people were to be respected, encouraged and admired for their endless hours of hard work, often for little to absolutely no money. For us "gray hairs" inside the campaign, that meant we were quietly expected to provide support, wisdom, leadership and mentorship.

3. The third thing I quickly understood was to ignore the laughs, jokes and outside background noise about how young people could not be relied on to get out and vote. After all, we knew better.

So I quickly learned the phone scripts, was able to read, repeat and explain Obama's policy positions on social, environmental, national security and other issues. And something else interesting was happening. I was repeatedly being mistaken for Michelle Obama. A typical phone exchange went something like this:

"Thank you for calling the Obama for America Campaign! This is Michelle. How may I help you?" (That would be me.)

"Michelle Obama?"

(Chuckle; faint blush) "Oh, no Ma'am, I'm another Michelle."

"Oh." (That would be the disappointed caller.)

And a bit later into the conversation, "You sure you're not Michelle Obama? You sorta sound like her."

(Chuckle, again.) "Yes Ma'am, I'm sure. I'm not Michelle Obama. I'm another Michelle."

And so it went. Under-over bets began to take place in the Call Center, to see not only would I be asked the question, but how many times. Usually within a four-hour work day, I'd be asked the "Michelle Obama?" question by at least three different callers. That phrase, "I'm another Michelle," got me to thinking – I really am "another Michelle." As my new life in Chicago began taking shape, and my mother's health was improving, I began feeling better, feeling new. And so gradually, I became known by other Call Center volunteers as "the other Michelle."

CHAPTER
Two
CAMPAIGN FUNDRAISERS
FUNDRAISING – FROM THE TOP DOWN

CARNIVALE – JUNE 8, 2007

Carnivale Restaurant is beautiful. Decorated in bold colors, artwork and painted fabric, the Latin restaurant was the host location for the $1,000-a-head Obama fundraiser. Sassy Latin music muscled its way through the overhead speakers. The food spread was divine – fresh fruit, veggies (including asparagus and eggplant), cheeses and breads, jumbo shrimp, lobster tails, scallops and crab legs. Waitstaff came by with sangrias, margaritas, mini-lamb chops, beef tenderloins and various tarts for dessert. The setting, beautiful. The night, magical.

I, along with about twenty staff and volunteers, were two hours early for the big event. My assignment was to mingle. *That I can do*, I said to myself. So a few other volunteers and I took off our badges and waited for the crowd to come so that we could mingle. It was still early, and we weren't letting people in yet. One of the first people to come in, though, was Jill Scott. It turned out that she wasn't part of the event. She and a young man walked and talked softly, seemingly looking over every inch of the place. Perhaps they were scoping out the place for a future venue for her. Had I not attended her concert the night before, I might not even have recognized her. The truth is I wasn't even sure it was actually her. As she approached my table, our eyes locked. We both smiled. She apparently thought I was someone important, because she headed straight towards me. Without the big, crinkly hair and glistening stage makeup, she looked just about like any other stout but pretty sista in the hood. I couldn't say with certainty that this woman was Jill Scott. Our eyes never left each other, as if asking, *Don't I know you from somewhere?* Her pace slowed as she reached the table. I spoke to her. She spoke back. I extended my hand and she shook it. I was mingling. I was shaking hands with this maybe-Jill Scott-maybe-not person and in the nervousness of the moment asked the stupidest question.

"Hey, were you at the Jill Scott concert last night at the Auditorium?"

She gave me a quizzical look that quickly turned into an indignant smirk that said, *Was I at the Jill Scott concert? Are you kidding me? I was the Jill Scott concert!*

She never actualized those words, but her look told me what a big blunder I'd just made. Being the professional that she is, she gently released my hand, whispered good-bye and carried on with her walk-through of the restaurant.

I felt silly, uncool even. I took solace in the fact that only she and I knew what had just happened. I collected myself, held my shoulders back and smiled at a handsome gentleman in a dark blue suit approaching our table, who seemed eager to mingle.

"Isn't she beautiful?" Senator Obama asked us.

"Yes!" we responded.

"Isn't she great?" he volleyed back.

"Yes!" we cheered.

"Well, you ain't seen nothing yet!" he teased.

We erupted in laughter and applause as Michelle Obama exited the staircase landing and disappeared behind the heavy drapes. She had just finished telling cute stories about Barack, the husband – about his dirty socks and his not hanging up his pants; about her battle to get him to pick up after himself or boil an egg just right. We laughed as she humanized the man. She spoke clearly, deliberately and was surprisingly funny. She was also absolutely stunning in a tea-length silk navy dress that was form-fitting with a stiff shawl collar that seemed to frame her regal face. She looked as if she'd stepped out of the pages of *Vogue* magazine. She had, in fact, just finished a photo shoot for the September issue.

Senator Obama took over the staircase landing turned stage and fired up the crowd. He spoke about his vision for the future of the nation, a vision of equality, opportunities and endless possibilities. He spoke about his mixed heritage of a father from Kenya and a mother from Kansas, and of being raised on three different continents. He talked about how these experiences growing up colored his view of the world and influenced his left-leaning politics. He shared some of his successes as a community organizer, including how he helped to register hundreds of thousands of new voters and how he helped the tenants of the Altgeld Gardens housing project fight against asbestos, lead-filled paint on their walls, and unclean water in their community. He spoke about legislative successes he'd enjoyed as a state senator in the Illinois legislature, which included providing health care monies for tens of thousands of poor women and children in Illinois, targeting an end to racial profiling and police abuse, and being a fierce advocate against the nonsensical war in Iraq.

The more he talked, the more I learned. The more I learned, the more I liked him. He ended with challenging us to look at his voting record as a state senator and now as a United States senator. He asked us for our votes and our support in fighting the mammoth political machine that embodied the Clintons and their supporters. Looking up at this man on that staircase landing, liking what I heard, feeling the joy and jubilance in the room, I knew at that moment that I'd made the right decision in backing this candidate for president. I smiled broadly and snapped a few more pictures before Barack said, "God bless you and God bless America," as he exited the staircase and disappeared into the crowd of supporters waiting at the base of the steps.

That was my first Obama campaign fundraising event. Many more would follow.

Breakfast at the Mid-Day Club – July 16, 2007

Three months into working at the NHQ, I had become a staple in the Call Center. Like clockwork, I was now there three days a week for a total of twelve hours. The campaign, and especially Liz, was appreciative of the volunteers who dedicated that sort of time. Since we weren't being paid for our time and skills, she'd give what she could – perks. The biggest perk was to be selected to volunteer at fundraising events where the senator himself was the headliner. I got a second opportunity on the 16th of July.

A select group of attorneys were hosting a Breakfast with Barack fundraiser at the Mid-Day Club located in the Chase Tower, with ticket prices starting at $500 per person. My admission fare: be one of the greeters at the registration table. There was one big drawback. I had to be there at 6:30 a.m. for the early morning event.

The fundraiser was held on the 56th floor of a private, members-only club for mostly law professionals. The club was old and beautiful. Rich woods filled the room, from walnut doors and crown moldings around the ceilings to rows and rows of mahogany and brass book-shelves. I greeted Becky, the contact person from the Finance Team, as I approached the two tables set up for registration. There were five of us total: three volunteers, one intern and Becky. Our required attire was business, so I donned a chocolate-colored skirt suit, stark white blouse, three-inch pumps and a brilliant smile. The check-in process included asking for names (with a smile), giving out preprinted name badges (with a smile), and issuing a bunch of thank-yous (with a smile). No problem. The truth is, it was fun. By 7 o'clock people started trickling in, and the lineup of attendees seemed straight out of the pages of old-money Chicago society tabloids: Penny Pritzker (the Hyatt heiress); William M. Daley (youngest brother of Mayor Richard M. Daley); John W. Rogers, Jr. (millionaire businessman, CEO of Ariel Investments); James S. Crown (president of Henry Crown and Company – a private investment company – and director of J. P. Morgan Chase & Co.); and the list went on.

The trickle of people became a rush, as we were chatting it up with some of the guests and escorted others to the dining area up the hall. Two soft-spoken, clean-shaven men of some professional distinction hung back behind the crowd. Lingering closely behind them was that unique yet nondescript smell of old money. You know, that scent, that fragrance, that air which smells rich and classic but can't be readily identified, the kind of scent which is custom-designed for that particular person, or family, or pedigree. This was the type of crowd that this event drew. The two men walked casually past registration, engaged in conversation, headed toward the dining room. Our assistance wasn't needed. They knew exactly where to go. They'd been here many times before. The rush subsided and suddenly it was quiet. I used the opportunity to really absorb my surroundings. Large panels of windows lined the east wall. Leather oxblood chairs flanked the windows with the morning sun glistening off the studs of their rolled arms. The high-up view of Lake Michigan hugging the shoulders of downtown Chicago was spectacular. *Wow!* I thought. *So this is what having a law degree, the right connections and a membership to a private bar association club feels like.*

One of the volunteers nudged me, shaking loose my thoughts. She leaned in and whispered, "He's in the building."

He didn't need to be explained. *He* was the person we were all up so early and waiting to hear speak. *He* was the candidate, Senator Barack Obama. My heart started beating a bit faster. I'd only seen the senator in person one time before. I was as nervous as on a first date.

I smiled at the volunteer and said, "Oh! Thanks."

Moments later, we could hear their footsteps before seeing anyone. Judging from the heaviness of the sound, there were a half dozen men walking our way. They rounded the corner, entered the lounge where we were, and I saw him: tall, slim, poised, polished. He smiled and stopped to talk to a few people lingering near the registration tables, placing a hand on a shoulder, looking the listener in the eyes. He really knew how to work a room full of big shots. And as he neared my table, he looked dead-on at me, too.

Extending his hand for a shake, looking me square in the eyes, he said, "Thank you very much."

I smiled and burped up something that resembled, "You're welcome, Senator."

He went down the line of volunteers and staff, giving us the same greeting and respect that he'd given his guests. *What a class act*, I thought.

Once he left the registration area and was clearly out of earshot, we collectively let out soft, schoolgirl giggles. We didn't have to say it. We all felt it. At that very moment, we were proud to be supporting this man and working this event. I wanted to hear what Senator Obama had to say, and Becky let us go to the dining area to listen and eat.

The room was huge, holding at least twenty table-rounds of eight. The smell of breakfast foods met us at the door and filled the air. White table linens draped row after row of six-foot buffet tables situated just beneath the wall of windows and Chicago skyline. Each buffet table made a different and equally tempting offer: a variety of stainless steel chafing dishes warmed the bacon, sausage, scrambled eggs and country hash browns on the hot foods table; the cold table held the milks and bottled water, orange and cranberry juices, fresh-cut fruit, whole bananas and yogurt on ice; the breads table contained muffins, toasts, danish rolls and granola bars; the hot-beverage table offered piping-hot regular and decaffeinated coffees, carafes of cream, and hot water for the large assortment of gourmet teas. I scanned the culinary parade and casually made my selections.

". . .And without further ado, ladies and gentlemen, here's Senator Barack Obama!"

To polite applause, the senator walked to the front of the room, queued up his wireless microphone and greeted his colleagues.

"Good morning! First off I'd like to thank Bill, say thanks to Penny and all of the good folks who put this event together. I have to also say thank you to all of you for coming out so early, for supporting and contributing to my campaign, and for wanting to hear my economic plan for the country. So. Let's talk."

Senator Obama began discussing his vision and plan for improving the economy, which included analyzing, cutting and balancing the budget.

". . .I won't cut the budget with an axe, but rather go line by line, item by item, with a scalpel and make the measured cuts where necessary."

More polite applause. The eggs on my plate were warmer than this tepid audience. As if oblivious to the spiritless response, Obama continued talking, ticking off his list of economic priorities.

"I want to grow our economy so that every American has a chance to succeed. Here's what I want to do:"

1. Give tax relief to 98 percent of households making less than $250,000 a year.
2. Give tax credits up to $1,000 for working families.
3. Raise the minimum wage to $9.50 per hour.
4. Save one million jobs.
5. Make health care affordable for all Americans.
6. Empower families to succeed by making college affordable for everyone.
7. Pay for all proposals.
8. Cut the deficit.
9. Cut government waste.
10. Eliminate special tax breaks for corporations.[5]

A short while later, Senator Obama opened the floor up for questions, and a barrage of not-so-polite questions hit him like flying spitballs:

"It's hard to get folks to give money to your campaign, Barack, when they don't know exactly where you stand on the issues! What should I be out here tellin' 'em?" a seemingly perturbed suited-and-booted man shouted from his front-and-center table.

"Same here," started another suit. "Broad goals sound good, but where's the beef, so to speak?"

"People are complaining about your lack of experience. How do I convince them that you're the real deal?" shouted another.

"Yeah, how do we counter the Hillary factor with women voters?"

And on and on the questions went, each one a bit more forceful and angry than the previous one. Senator Obama took each question seriously. He'd pivot to his right or left to look the questioner in the face and allow the person to get his question out before answering. The one answer I remember vividly was when he said something along these lines:

---

[5] This list of economic priorities is as I remember them at that event, and later verified in the following: Obama For America, "Reviving Our Economy: Strengthening The Middle Class," Change We Can Believe In, New York: Three Rivers Press, 2008, pp. 27-59.

"I don't expect you guys to remember all of my policy positions on issues, but you can remember my web address where all my policy positions are laid out for anyone to read. You can tell people that!

"And if that's not good enough, there's a toll-free number to my national headquarters with trained, professional volunteers at the ready to answer questions. You can tell people that!

"And if that's not good enough, you can give them my cell number. You all have it. So. If you or your trusted friends have questions, call me. Thank you everybody!"

And with a wave of the hand, he was off the stage and on the floor shaking hands and confirming his cell number. His comeback answers had been confident and courageous. This was the first time I'd seen a combative Obama, where his smile disappeared and eyes grew dark. His verbal boxing skills were classic Muhammad Ali (both the boxer and orator). Obama was gracious, with verbal punches that moved as silently as breath, stopping the opponent cold in his tracks.

Yes, the more I saw and heard from this man, the more he had my support.

PIZZA PARTY AT THE NHQ – JULY 19, 2007

Liz invited us all to a "staff-and-volunteer pizza party" to be held on Thursday, July 19th. I worked on Thursdays, and free food is almost always extra tasty, so it was a no-brainer. I was in. I called my friend Cynthia to let her know about the event, trying to convince her that it would be fun, but to no avail. Her answer was, "I'll pass."

About four o'clock that afternoon, NHQ staff and volunteers started filing into the meeting room. The sights and smells were delicious. There were rows and rows of pizzas: cheese, deep-dish cheese and sausage, pepperoni, and vegetarian. Another table held varieties of sodas, diet sodas, bottled water, cups and ice, and the dessert table held a variety of Eli's cheesecakes: plain, chocolate swirl, strawberry-topped, caramel and crushed nuts.

We filed in and took seats at the tables of our choice. I sat next to a young brother who was a volunteer in the Design and Production

Department. The party officially opened with welcomes and thank yous from staff in campaign manager David Plouffe's and campaign assistant manager Steve Hildebrand's offices. About a hundred of us convened there. The just-got-off-work crowd began showing up. People came with their children and grandchildren, and we played a bit of musical chairs to allow newcomers a chance to sit down and eat.

I'd just finished my pizza and 7-Up and was headed for the caramel-and-nuts cheesecake on the dessert table when I saw her: Michelle Obama. She was tall, even in her low-heeled, black ballerina shoes. She wore a white cotton blouse over black khaki pedal pushers, no hosiery, a broad smile. She didn't quite look the same as her photo images. She looked tired. And no wonder, barreling out in front of her was Sasha, a happy-go-lucky kid with cute dimples and pigtails in chaos after a long day at play.

I nudged the person standing next to me and said, "Look, Michelle Obama!"

He was a young, East Indian-looking guy, who smiled and said, "Sure is, what a surprise, huh?"

What a surprise is right. They didn't tell us that she would there. *Was he going to be there too?* I wondered. I grabbed my handy camera and waited for Michelle to make her way towards my end of the room. It seemed as if I'd turned away for a second, and then, bam! there she was.

"I love your shoes," she said, smiling down at me.

"Oh, thanks," I nervously chuckled, looking down at my black patent leather mules with woven straw vamps.

She asked my name and I told her, Michelle. I told her that I volunteered in the Call Center and nearly every time I worked, a caller would ask if I was Michelle Obama. This time she chuckled, and quick-wittedly responded with, "Like I'm the only Michelle working the campaign."

We both chuckled and I asked her for a photograph. She agreed and pulled me close to her for us to take a photograph together. I handed the camera to the East Indian guy standing near me, and he snapped the shot – the first in my series of "Michelle" shots.

I thanked her as she moved on to shake more hands and take more pictures. I rushed outside and downstairs for a smoke and to call Cynthia.

"Hey, Cynthia! Gir-r-rlll, you missed it!" I screamed into the phone.

"Missed what?"

"The pizza party!"

"What happened?" she asked.

"Two words: Michelle. Obama."

October 29, 2007

Dear Journal,

I've met the most wonderful man. His name is James. He's one of the most interesting and intelligent men that I've met in a long time. He's different in so many ways, the least of which is his Norwegian descent. But, he's a white guy who gets it; who apologizes for slavery and the pain that it causes on both sides of the aisle. He's tall, slim, long hair, soft brown eyes – oh, and did I mention plenty sexy!

He's in the adult education field, which is cool within itself, but he's also the lead guitarist and singer in a band! I like this guy. He seems to like me, too. I spent this past Sunday in Evanston with him. We talked and drank, walked downtown, held hands. This, much like the Obama campaign, looks very promising.

My prayer today is:

Dear Heavenly Father,
Please continue to use me for the purposes that you see fit;
And bless me and Mom with good health, peace, happiness, and love.
In Jesus' name, I pray.
Amen."

ೞ

FUNDRAISING — FROM THE GROUND UP

As with any other presidential campaign, fundraising at the national level was a big part of the Obama presidential campaign, too. Big-ticket events, parties, luncheons, and other opportunities for handshaking and schmoozing were vital to getting the necessary revenues to keep the campaign humming. When Senator Obama wasn't fundraising, Michelle Obama was. He did the big-ticket events. She did the small ones. One such event was held on the South Side of Chicago at the Grand Ballroom on Cottage Grove Avenue. It was a hot, August day, and the ballroom was packed. Tickets were only $25 each, so people came. Everyday people filled the place: working folks; young hip-hoppers in athletic jerseys and sagging jeans; Gray Panthers in church crowns and on walking sticks; people of color from the hood; lakefront liberals from the north shore of Evanston and south shore liberals from Hyde Park. There was standing room only. The ballroom was hot, Michelle's message was fiery, the event – electric.

As the Obamas stumped on the campaign trail, monies flowed in from both formal fundraising events and small online contributions. To help boost the small fundraising, the campaign birthed a brain child called the "grassroots finance committee" (GFC).

"Hey, Michelle. You know Chris Hughes?" Liz asked casually.
"No."
"Well, he's the director of the my.barackobama.com website."
"Okay?"
"You don't know Chris Hughes? The Facebook Guy? Well anyway, he's forming a grassroots fundraising group and asked if I could recommend some staff and volunteers for the committee."
"Uh-huh."
"I think you'll be great." She said with a smile
"Oh, I don't know about raising money, Liz."
"Come on. You'll be great. So, I'll give him your contact info." She said with a raised brow, "Okay?"

"Okay." I caved.

And so I was in. Into what, I had no idea. I was just going with the flow. After all, the Facebook Guy was in charge. How bad could it be?

The first GFC meeting was held at the National Headquarters in October 2007. I, along with a small group of volunteers, met with Chris Hughes and other members of the Social Networking Unit of the New Media Department. Chris Hughes was not only a Harvard graduate and one of three cofounders of the Facebook social networking company, but he was outright nice. He was a small-framed man with a thin waistline, bone-straight blond hair and a warm, broad smile that lit up his boyish face. I liked him immediately. He was the director of the my.barackobama.com website, or MyBO, as we called it. Chris sat the small group gathered and briefed us on the role of the GFC, and gave us folders filled with forms, strategies and other information to help us raise money.

This was the setup:

- The Grassroots Finance Committee (GFC) would be a ground-level mirror image of the National Finance Committee (NFC), which was chaired by Hyatt Hotels billionaire heiress Penny Pritzker. Our committee would be chaired by Chris Hughes, the billionaire social-networking genius with a penchant for bringing people together for a common cause.

- Just as Ms. Pritzker would use her national connections and social might to get big donors to participate in the campaign, Chris would use his creation, the MyBO website, to give us a platform to solicit and accept donations, to share information, to create personal profiles, and to monitor our personal fundraising meters. But mainly, being a part of the GFC gave us legitimacy and the fortitude to ask people to give money to the campaign.

- While the NFC comprised dedicated wealthy supporters from across the country, the GFC comprised dedicated volunteers of every professional stripe.

- The NFC would focus on big-ticket events that cost hundreds to thousands of dollars per person. Each member of this massive committee of 250-plus people would be responsible for raising tens of thousands of dollars for the campaign, bringing their fundraising goal into the tens of millions.[6] The GFC would focus on donations as small as five dollars. Our initial group totaled 200 people nationwide, each committed to raising at least a thousand dollars, giving us a fundraising goal of $200,000.

- Just as the NFC did, we would meet weekly via conference calls to share strategies, encourage each other, and tally up the weekly haul.

- Unlike the NFC, our committee would only be in place for a three-month period from October through December 2007, with the one goal: to raise money to aid the soon-to-be-deployed ground forces for the upcoming "get-out-the-caucus" (GOTC) campaign in Iowa.

We were supplied with forms, stickers, policy information, and names and contact information of staff to call, all intended to assist us if we got stuck answering questions, as well as to ease our nervousness, unsurety, or cases of outright cold feet. One of the most helpful handouts provided listed just how the small donations would be used by the campaign:

1. $5 – buys 7 supporter cards used to sign up Iowans who pledge to caucus for Barack.
2. $10 – buys 10 packets of hand warmers for volunteers and field organizers going door-to-door in below-freezing temperatures.
3. $20 – buys 155 Obama lapel stickers for caucus night (one precinct's worth).
4. $50 – buys 20 reams of paper to print final precinct walk and call lists.
5. $100 – buys 10 pizzas for high school volunteers.
6. $500 – buys 1 week of printer toner for GOTC offices in Iowa.
7. $1,000 – buys 20 precincts' worth of hot chocolate to keep our

---

[6] A complete listing of the members of the Obama for America National Finance Committee can be found at: http://www.gwu.edu/~action/2008/obama/obamaorggen.html; click on the "Finance" link, and then click on "National Finance Committee" under Penny Pritzker's name.

supporters warm as they wait in line at their respective precinct caucuses.

8. $2,300 – buys one month's rent and utilities for a local field office.
9. $10,000 – buys 76,000 door-hangers that tell supporters their caucus location.
10. $50,000 – buys two weeks of online advertising in Iowa.
11. $100,000 – buys one week of radio advertising in Iowa.
12. $250,000 – buys one week of television advertising in Iowa.

By our next meeting in November, Chris was proud to announce that we were well on our way to reaching our $200,000 goal. In fact, we were nearly halfway there with $77,000 raised. He asked us to share how we each raised money. So we did. Some people held bake sales. Others conducted car washes. One couple did a walk-a-thon. I threw a house party and raised $230.

The next time that I worked at the Call Center, I brought in a large manila envelope filled with donation slips, checks, credit card vouchers and yes, cash. Emily Boker, one of the workers on Chris's team, looked inside the envelope and smiled. She raised an eyebrow as if to ask, *Do I really want to know?*

I shook my head and said, "No, you don't want to know."

We chuckled, not so much at the Chicago-gangster-implied-joke, but at the fact that the GFC had begun as an idea that was now working and netting real money. We took an unspoken pride in that and shared a laugh about it.

By the end of December, the GFC had surpassed the goal of $200,000 and had collectively raised $275,000. Not bad for three months' work from people who were not skilled fundraisers. It also was not a bad haul to help the field operations in Iowa.

༄

National fundraising events were happening fast and furious, bringing high-profile visitors in and out of the headquarters on a near-daily basis. On one occasion I saw Dr. Cornel West, of Princeton University fame. He nodded, waved and flashed a smile as he toured the head-quarters. On another occasion, I saw Dr. Randal Pinkett, the black guy who'd won the fourth season of Donald Trump's television show *The Apprentice*. He also smiled and waved as he passed through. By the end of December, I'd seen more famous faces than I can remember, if not at the headquarters, then at local fundraising events. Three such events are especially memorable.

IDLEWILD COUNTRY CLUB ~ FLOSSMOOR, IL – NOVEMBER 18, 2007

I became a member of South Suburban Women for Obama, a volunteer fundraising and get-out-the-vote group composed primarily of women who lived in the south suburbs of Chicago. This group was headed by Angela Lewis, the wife of Michelle Obama's (and her brother Craig Robinson's) former elementary school principal, Dr. Robert Lewis. The group cosponsored a fundraiser with Tim Bradford, a committee-man from Rich Township. The tickets were working-man-priced at $25, $50, $100 and $500 per person. Michelle Obama was the headliner.

A live band, The Voices, kicked off the event with smooth sounds of the Temptations, Stylistics and other groups from the seventies. Michelle was late coming out on stage, because she and Tim Bradford had been backstage "stepping" to the sweet sounds of the music. She came out smiling broadly.

"Hello, Chicago-o-o!" She beamed. "It's so good to be home! And boy, was that band the greatest or what? This is the first event ever that I've had a chance to do a little bit of stepping before coming onstage!"

She knew how to warm up a crowd. The audience roared.

The South Suburban Women group were sitting front and center, but every now and again I looked over at my delegation of friends and family who'd come to hear Michelle speak: my mother (Doris Levy) and her longtime friend, Mrs. Lillian Wallace, both dressed to the nines in sequins and snazzy pumps; my high school and college friends, Denise, Rosalyn Jamison (Mickey), and Cheryl Douthard; Don Baird, a cowork-er from the college; and lastly, my potential new beau, James Edwards.

He coolly sat and listened and laughed or clapped or smiled whenever appropriate. Michelle told funny stories about home life with Barack, about how they met, and about how she didn't want to be bothered with him at first. She then quickly added:

". . .But, I did good didn't I?"

"You sure did, girl!" we hooted and hollered back.

She smoothly moved on to talking about what Barack had done for women and children especially, as a community organizer, then as a state senator, and what he was trying to do now as U. S. senator. Finally she talked about why he felt compelled to run for president.

"Just imagine a world where your sons and my daughters are attending schools where they're truly being taught, and trained, to be whatever they can imagine themselves being; and imagine a government that works, that's responsive to the needs of the people; and imagine a place where food is clean and nutritious and doesn't cause obesity; and hospitals that heal the sick at an affordable cost.

"Now, imagine that there is one person who has the heart and intellect and energy to help make all of these things work the way they're supposed to; a person who is qualified to do the job and do it right. Except, he doesn't look like the person you've just imagined. Could you accept the truth from such a person? Could you accept the truth no matter how it was packaged?

"We all know the truth when we hear it. We know it when we see it. We know it when we feel it. Suppose the truth came packaged as Barack Obama? Could you accept it? Would you accept it?

"I'm asking you to support him, to support the truth. Will you help us? Will you help us win? Folks, Chicago, I'm asking for your vote. Can we count on you?"

The audience sat quiet, that stunned, contemplative kind of quiet when mulling serious questions. And as we realized that she was finished, a ripple of ovations exploded with shouts and clapping and whistling.

"Yes, we'll help!" people yelled in response.

"You go, girl!"

"Yes! Yes!" A few supporters began stirring the crowd.

"Homerun, Michelle!"

"Yes! Yes! Yes, we can! Yes! Yes! Yes, we can!"

That evening we raised a few thousand dollars and signed up dozens of new volunteers. And for the second time, I took a picture with the future first lady.

SOUTH SHORE CULTURAL CENTER ~ CHICAGO, IL NOVEMBER 30, 2007

April Harley from the Finance Department called to ask if I could volunteer for an event. *Hell, yeah*, I thought.

"Of course!" I said, without asking any of the particulars.

She then asked if I could also get three of my friends to volunteer for the event.

"Of course!" I repeated.

I wasn't sure if I could or not, but I wasn't going to pass up the opportunity to get some of my friends involved firsthand in this historic campaign. Within an hour, I had rounded up three reliable friends whom I personally knew and trusted, and who were also Obama supporters. Two days later we were at the South Shore Cultural Center, where the event took place.

This was a big-ticket fundraising event being sponsored by Michelle Obama's "girls," including: Desiree Rogers (a public relations executive and former wife of millionaire businessman John W. Rogers, Jr.); Staci R. Collins Jackson (Director of Corporate Affairs at Johnson Publishing Company); Shawnelle Richie (Director of Community Affairs at CBS Corporation, Chicago); and many others. This was a special event at a special place, where the Obamas had held their wedding reception. Being such, I and my "girls," Denise, Mickey and Diretha Lavizzo, showed up dressed to the hilt in every variation of black, trimmed in gold lamé, faux fur, sequins or something that indicated we were attending a big-time, after-five event.

Denise and Diretha worked the coat check. Mickey and I were greeters at the entrance doors to the ballroom. At six o'clock sharp, people started coming. It was a showcase of Chicago's African American who's who: women with diamonds the size of small lumps of coal; older sistas looking absolutely regal in indigo-colored West African mud-cloth suits, coordinating hand-hammered metal earrings, cuffs and chokers; younger sistas high-stepping in high-heeled suede boots, short glittery dresses, no hosiery and broad smiles. The parade of glitz and glamor continued for over an hour before Michelle Obama came down the staircase from a private reception. She wore simple clothes: a gray knit dress that hugged her athletic frame, black suede boots with skinny heels, white pearls and a wide smile. She headed my way as she entered the ballroom. She smiled and shook my hand as she passed. She stopped, turned and looked at me again, as if asking, *"Hey, haven't I seen you somewhere before?"* She stepped back, spoke again and then gave me a big bear hug.

She and her entourage entered the ballroom, and so did we. Michelle and "her girls" were on the dance floor doing the Electric Slide. "My girls" and I danced where we were standing and enjoyed being a part of the moment. We were partying with Michelle and her friends, and in doing so felt as if we were now part of her "girls" too.

She gave a powerful and impassioned speech, much of what I'd heard at other events. So Denise, Mickey, Diretha and I didn't stay in the ballroom to hear it all, but headed out to the coatroom to prepare for the onslaught of people wanting their winter wraps. Michelle Obama came out of the ballroom, stopping along the way to take pictures. Of our group, Diretha got one first; then Denise posed for a picture with her; then Denise took one of me and Michelle; then I noticed that Mickey wasn't around. *She's in the bathroom,* I thought. I ran to get her. I opened the bathroom door and yelled, "Hey Mickey! Michelle is taking pictures! Cut it off if you have to!"

Mickey and I raced back to the coatroom area just in time for Michelle Obama's security to announce that she wasn't taking any more pictures. Mickey and I gave her the saddest looks, asked if she could take just one more – for Mickey's two young daughters. Michelle looked at our sad faces and probably thought about her own daughters. We must have tugged at her heart, because she waved Mickey forward to take one last picture. They both looked beautiful, Mickey in her black, Michelle in her gray, their smiles glistening bright white. Michelle's security whisked her off to an awaiting car, and we all smiled and laughed and hugged and high-fived, realizing almost simultaneously that we may have just hugged and taken pictures with the future First Lady.

SECOND CITY THEATRE ~ CHICAGO, IL – DECEMBER 07, 2007

Barack Obama was the showcase guest at the renowned Second City Theatre, where many of the Saturday Night Live cast got their start. A $750-per-person event titled "Between Barack and a Hard Place" was being held there. My coworker, Dr. Donald Baird, had bought a ticket through my campaign fundraising site, pulling my grassroots fundraising total over $1,540. I was offered an opportunity to volunteer at this event, and unlike me, I arrived about twenty minutes late. All of the assignments had been given out. I badly wanted to be part of this event. I started sweating and becoming panicky. I was mad at myself for being late. I spotted April Harley and explained what had happened. She offered a sympathetic look and apologized, explaining that this was Jordan's event, so he'd have to okay whether or not I could still work.

Jordan Kaplan, a young, dark haired, type-A financial whiz, was not the world's most approachable guy. He was also the director of the Illinois Finance Department. I looked in his direction. He was talking to a guy and simultaneously punching something into his Blackberry. That was Jordan. You rarely got his full attention. I sighed and accepted that my chances of getting in were somewhere between slim to none. I squared my shoulders as I approached him.

"Hey, Jordan!" I greeted him nervously.

Looking up momentarily from his Blackberry, he answered absently, "Hey."

"Um, I was just explaining to April that I, uh, was scheduled to volunteer at this event."

"Yeah?"

"Well, I got caught in traffic and got here too late to get an assignment."

"Uh-huh, 'cuse me," he said, slightly turning his back towards me to take a call.

I stood with my hands behind my back, knees locked to prevent fidgeting my feet, feeling like a grade school kid trying to appeal to an overworked, irritated principal. Jordan ended his call and seemed a bit surprised that I was still standing there. He gave me a quizzical look, somewhere between "oh-you're-still-standing-here" and "I-can't-believe-your-nerve-lady." I seized upon the vulnerability of his surprise and the momentary silence of his Blackberry to quickly continue my story.

"I'm sorry to be late, but I can work wherever you need me." I waited a moment and added, "I came from the far South Side and the traffic was really rough. I. . ."

He cut me off mid-sentence and placed his hand on my shoulder. "Sorry we gotcha out in the rain," he said.

Oh, boy, I thought. *Here it comes.*

"Don't worry about working tonight," Jordan continued.

I knew it, I said to myself.

"Come on in and enjoy the show," he added and smiled briefly before his phone rang and he punched a button on his Blackberry, slightly turning his back again and took the call.

I couldn't believe it. Not only was I in, but I wasn't even working. I was now a guest, a spectator, a pretend donor. I also couldn't believe that Jordan had smiled. I told him thanks. He didn't hear me. His attention was on his call. I move quickly towards the auditorium door, in part because I was happy, and in part because I didn't want Jordan to end his call and change his mind.

I stood in the short line that was forming and waited my turn to be seated. I was led to a two-person table in the front row. I literally could reach out and touch the stage. I placed my purse in the other seat and began looking out for Don. I spotted him and waved. He came over and was instantly impressed that I'd snagged such premium seats. Waitstaff served us appetizers of grilled shrimp kebobs, fried shrimp tempura, chicken teriyaki, parmesan cheese bread, free drinks and more. And just as the staff stopped serving, the lights lowered and the show began.

Hilarious comedians of all races one after another represented a different segment of the voting population. They poked fun at the many issues that had arisen during the campaign:

- The gay comedian pined about Barack's celebrity and attractiveness, *"Oh, ain't he fine, though?"*
- The white male comedian played Barack channeling the ghost of Abraham Lincoln.
- The black female comedian wrung her hands and rapped in rhyme the chants of older black women's fear for this "sweet little boy's" safety.
- The young white female comedian played a rough-and-tumble Hillary Clinton, plotting to hurt or maybe even bump off this *"pesky little candidate who came from out of nowhere."*

We clapped and laughed hard, but when they presented Barack Obama, the small theatre exploded with jubilance.

Obama's speech was peppered with humor as he poked fun at himself and the comedians. He thanked us for our support and donations and hard work. He asked that we hang in there and go the extra mile for the fight in Iowa. His tone became serious as he shared his vision for a more equal America; a more engaged America; and an America that would see herself as part of the larger world-society. We interrupted his speech several times with ovations and applause. Afterwards, he worked the front row, smiling, shaking hands, patting shoulders, taking pictures. Don and I shook his hand and beamed with excitement.

Once the event was over, I drove away in a daze, reflecting on this night with Barack Obama. I glided my car through the rain-slicked, sleeping streets of Chicago and headed home. I reflected on how I'd started my day kissing the lips of the man I'd come to love – James, and ended it with shaking the hand of the man I'd come to admire – Barack. What a perfect ending to a perfect start. I drove home in complete silence, alone with my thoughts, thinking — *Next stop, Iowa!*

Early on Obama supporters attending a fundraiser at the Idlewild Country Club in Flossmoor, Illinois, November 18, 2007: (l to r) Denise Snyder, Cheryl Douthard, Doris Levy (Mom) and longtime family friend, Lillian Wallace.

Me and my friends are all smiles with Michelle Obama, after volunteering at a fundraiser at the South Shore Cultural Club, November 30, 2007.

Me and the future First Lady at the NHQ pizza party in July 2007!

December 26, 2007

Dear Journal,

Today I head out for the 9-day "Get-Out-The-Caucus" ground work for the Obama campaign. I've packed my new coat with faux fur, borrowed caps and hiking boots from Denise and her family, as well as an Escada Pour Homme cologne-scented knit scarf from James. My hotel confirmation is in my purse. Clare, a young college kid who lives in the Beverly neighborhood, is coming to scoop me up for our four-hour drive to Iowa City, Iowa.

Just hugged Mom good-bye and gave her a lingering kiss on the cheek. I saw the concerned look on her face and the shadow of tears that she was holding back. I gave her an extra squeeze, just to let her know that I'd be okay. I believe in Barack Obama. I believe in the work that I am doing for the campaign. I believe Mom believes this too. So, here it is 6:30 in the morning on the day after Christmas. Most people are probably still turning over in their warm beds. I'm wide-eyed and anticipating the next nine days. I'm dressed. I'm packed. I'm fired up and ready to go!

My prayer today is:

"Dear Heavenly Father,
Please continue to use me for the purposes that you see fit;
And bless me and Mom with good health, happiness, love and longevity.
In Jesus' name, I pray.
Amen."

CHAPTER

Three

IOWA

THE CAUCUS PROCESS

The drive to Iowa was uneventful, with typical Midwestern winter scenery: flat, grazed, snow-covered cornfields. We reached Iowa City about 10:30 a.m. Surprisingly, it was beautiful and hilly. A quaint, small town wrapped around the University of Iowa. Volunteers from across the country began arriving. The largest contingency was from Chicago. The room buzzed with excitement and apprehension and questioning looks that asked, *What have I gotten myself into?* Or, *Can I really make a difference?*

We were all issued training packets that contained information on how the Iowa caucuses work; scripts for our mock caucus role-play; sample voter sheets; and contact information for the Iowa leadership team. Everyone there was a volunteer. Most people were new to grassroots political involvement, so they listened intently as the leadership team explained the caucus process. I halfway tuned in. I was a political science major in undergraduate school and cut my political activist teeth more than three decades earlier during the Jimmy Carter presidential campaign. I knew the difference between a primary and a caucus. I knew how a caucus worked. I even understood the strategy behind making Iowa the first state to vote. So I looked around the room instead.

There were young people with bright eyes and old ones with stoic faces; athletic types in slick jogging suits, as well as people in wheelchairs; there were blacks, whites, and those in between whose race couldn't quite be distinguished just by looking at them; there were people with name tags that read Anne and Miguel and Rahman and Henry and William and Brandon and Sarah and of course, me, Michelle. People had come from near and far to be a part of this process and to learn how to do it correctly. My eyes locked in on the banner behind the speaker. "Respect. Empower. Include." That was the motto and mantra of the campaign. I decided to be a bit more respectful and listened in.

HOW THE CAUCUS WORKS

Over and over throughout the early part of the campaign, I was asked, "What is a caucus?" "How does a caucus work?" "Why does Iowa have caucuses instead of primaries?" "Is it fair for this little bitty state to have this much influence in a presidential election?" All of these questions ticked through my head as the Iowa leadership team took ample time to explain the what's, why's, and how's of the Iowa caucus process. It went something like this:

What Is a Caucus?

- Although commonly referred to as "a gathering of neighbors," the definition given by Iowa Caucus Project 2008 is: "The word caucus is a North American Indian word, thought to be of Algonquin origin, meaning a gathering of the ruling tribal chiefs."[7] Its modern meaning, however, includes the following:
  - ° A meeting of the local members of a political party especially to select delegates to a convention or register preferences for candidates running for office.
  - ° A closed meeting of party members within a legislative body to decide on questions of policy or leadership.
  - ° A group within a legislative or decision-making body seeking to represent a specific interest or influence a

---

[7] Iowa Caucus 2008, http://www.iowacaucus.org/iacaucus.html, paragraph three.

particular area of policy: a minority caucus.[8]

Why Does Iowa Have Caucuses Versus a Primary Election?

- Since the early 1800s (even before Iowa became a state), some form of caucus has existed. The early pioneers of the Iowa constitution chose caucuses rather than a primary to nominate candidates, preferring the grassroots, democracy-in-action approach.[9]

- Caucuses also work well for small communities in small states, especially when the populace is homogeneous, like Iowa. With a little over 3 million people, it has one of the nation's smallest populations, of which 90 percent (or 2.7 million) are white (non-Hispanic); 4 percent are Hispanic; 3 percent are black; and 2 percent are other.[10] Because we don't have direct elections of the president in America, but rather elections of delegates in primary elections and of an Electoral College for general elections, caucuses and primaries are conducted *not* to elect specific candidates, but to elect delegates to vote for our candidates of choice. For the 2008 presidential election, the first Democratic candidate to garner 2,116 delegates wins the party's nomination. Because the number of delegates allocated to a state is based on its population, Iowa is apportioned 57 delegates. This amount is small compared to 183 delegates from Illinois; 187 from Pennsylvania; 282 from New York State; and a whopping 441 from California. To make up for its slight delegate numbers, the Democratic Party has strengthened Iowa's voting power by placing it first in line for electing presidents.

How Does a Caucus in Iowa Work?

- Any voter who is a registered Democrat can participate in the Iowa Democratic caucus.

- Voters can also register or change their party affiliation at the door of the caucus.

[8] Iowa quick facts from the U. S. Census Bureau, http://quickfacts.census.gov/qfd/states/

[9] Iowa Caucus 2008, http://www.iowacaucus.org/iacaucus.html, paragraph three.

[10] Iowa quick facts from the U. S. Census Bureau, http://quickfacts.census.gov/qfd/states/ 19000.html.

- All caucus-goers meet in public buildings, such as schools or city halls, in their respective precincts.
- They must then divide themselves into groups, with each group representing a candidate.
- Voting is then publicly done, usually with a show of hands.
- Those votes (raised hands) are counted, and the determination of whether a candidate is viable is made.
- A candidate is viable if he or she receives at least 15 percent of the total caucus-goers' votes.
- If a candidate receives less than 15 percent of the caucus-go ers' votes in the "first round," then supporters of the non-via ble candidate(s) have 30 minutes to either join a viable candidate's group; join another non-viable candidate's group to try to make that candidate viable; join an uncommitted group; or choose not to be counted.
- Once this realignment has taken place, a second vote is taken. This "second round" of vote counting determines the winner of that precinct as well as the number of delegates pledged to support specific candidates during the county, state and national conventions.[11]

To illustrate the point of how caucuses work, the Iowa leadership team had us conduct a mock caucus. I was in the group voting for candidate Oprah. Others groups of candidates were Will Smith, Steven Spielberg, Barbara Streisand and Tom Sorensen. There were 6 delegates up for grabs. In the end, candidate Oprah had only enough votes to get 1 delegate. Candidate Smith got 2 delegates, because his vote percentage of 6 delegates was 1.57 which rounded up to 2. Candidate Oprah's vote percentage of 6 delegates was 1.38, which rounded down to 1. The difference in the size of our two groups was 2 people. This interactive exercise showed us the power of how persuading just one voter really matters.

We gathered our papers and notes and began to disseminate to our

---

[11] Gill, Kathy (2008). "How Do The Iowa Caucuses Work?" About.com US Politics. About: http://uspolitics.about.com/ad/2008elections/tp/how_caucuses_work.htm.

assigned Iowa cities. Clare, whom I'd ridden to Iowa City with, was assigned to stay there. I was stationed in Cedar Rapids. I hitched a ride with a guy named Adam to the Super 8 – Cedar Rapids, and on my way to spending the next nine days canvassing in Iowa.

HITTING THE STREETS OF IOWA

I was assigned to work out of a "station house" in Marion, Iowa. An elderly couple named Carol and Elden had a large, beautiful home with a sprawling backyard from which our operations were run. Carol had chocolate-covered pretzels, hot coffee and cocoa waiting. Doug, our coordinator, provided us with canvass packets and more training. Most people there had never done door-to-door canvassing for a campaign, so they sat wide-eyed, listening attentively. We had been told that this particular precinct had a lot of delegates, which made the responsibility of winning the precinct all the more heavy and made some people seem that much more nervous. I got paired up with a guy named Bob, who looked more nervous than I felt.

Up until that point, I had ignored, or accepted, that I was the only black person on the team and knew that what I was about to do was larger than me or my fear and apprehension. I was there representing a lot of people. I was there for my friends; for my family; for black folks in general; for folks on the South Side of Chicago in particular. It didn't matter that I was about to do something I hadn't ever done before in my life – me, a black woman in a small Midwestern nearly all-white town, knocking on the doors of total strangers and asking them to get out and publicly vote for a black man for U.S. President. At that moment, I could feel the greatness and importance of the time. I quickly, silently said a prayer for courage, tightened my coat around me, and hopped in the van with Bob.

Bob was a 53-year-old police officer who lived near the neighborhood where we canvassed. He was a bit more nervous than he should have been. He was more than just nervous. He seemed downright scared. We'd been instructed to each take our canvass sheets and one person take the odd side of the street and the other take the even. But once parked outside of the first address, Bob nervously suggested that "maybe we should just stick together," because it was getting dark outside. I agreed and said okay, but actually found his request a bit odd. *We could double our time if we split up, couldn't we?* I thought. *Why is this guy acting so nervous? After all, these are his neighbors, right? He should actually know some of these people.* And it struck me. He does. He does know these people. He does realize the weight of the situation. We weren't in a dangerous community – not violent, but we were in a delicate situation. The rubber was meeting the road.

I suddenly could hear my many conversations with James about the "racism of ignorance" versus the "racism of hatred." He had often told me about how Northern whites suffered from a type of racism of the ignorance of black people, while Southern whites suffered from racism of hatred. At that moment, sitting in Bob's van, I realized how racism had impacted us all – both blacks and whites. He was nervous not only for working a campaign for the first time, but he was nervous for me, and at the same time seemed ashamed that we both had to silently contemplate race and race relations in America. I realized at that moment that what I was doing was all the more important and had to be done; that we, Americans, have to end this madness; that we have to put *this* man at *this* time in *this* office. So, I looked over at Bob, giving him my million-dollar smile and said, "Okay we'll stick together. Let's do this."

By the end of the canvass, Bob and I had knocked on forty-three house, condo and apartment doors. We'd trekked across snow and ice, with flashlights and campaign literature in hand, and even though our hands were gloved, our fingers were ice cold. We felt we had done pretty good and smiled and took pictures to capture the moment of turning in our canvass sheets. At the end of that day, I was tired. I'd been up since four o'clock that morning and it was now after eight o'clock at night. My feet were hurting. My thighs and buttocks were stinging with soreness from getting in and out of a van over and over and over again, some forty-something times. My spirit was unsettled. The euphoria of the morning was gone. The hype dissipated, and I'd come to learn what the media referred to as "Iowa nice" really means.

It's that phony kind of nice, the "polite society" nice, and in my neighborhood, what we call "white folks nice" – the kind of "nice" that won't call you a nigger to your face; the kind of "nice" that wouldn't dare say to you, "The audacity of you, ringing my doorbell at night," but would think it; the kind of shielded "nice" that still can't quite cover that look of disdain for you being on their doorsteps, as they pleasantly say, "No, I'm still undecided, but thanks for the literature anyway." And although the overwhelming majority of people seemed to be genuinely nice, there were enough of the "white folks nice" around to make me feel it. I never felt threatened or in danger for my life or anything like that. I wasn't even treated badly, but at the end of that day, I knew I was a black woman in a small, white town in America with enough courage to – and yes, audacity – to stand up and try to make a change. As I buttoned my coat to leave the station house, I thought about Barack and Michelle Obama and thought about their incredible fortitude and resolve and admired them all the more. They had been out here for eleven months. I had experienced one cold winter's night.

I tightly wrapped James's scarf around my neck. I could smell his fragrance. I could smell his hair. I felt enveloped in him. That comforted me. I had a piece of familiarity with me – a piece of home. I inhaled the vapors in the night air and waved good-bye to Carol and Elden. A young man named Matt drove me back to the hotel. During the ride, I kept thinking and asking myself if I had made a difference? Had I done any good? Perhaps for the young lady who really wanted to vote for Oprah Winfrey but said that she would caucus for Obama anyway. Perhaps for the woman who was impressed by the fact that one of the senator's constituents had driven out from Chicago to canvass in Iowa. Perhaps. I'll never really know for sure. I could only hope.

$\wp$

The Scary, The Crazy, The Funny – Canvassing Trips in Iowa

The next day started early, mainly because I didn't sleep well the night before. I was scheduled to make phone calls from the Lynch Dallas Law Office near downtown Cedar Rapids, asking voters to caucus for Obama. The calls started out well enough – pleasant "No, thank you's" or "Yes, I'm going to caucus for Obama." Shortly thereafter came the hang-ups and "Take me off your d*mn list!" At the end of a four-hour shift of that, canvassing didn't seem so bad.

The next four hours was devoted to canvassing. I was teamed up with Bob again. This time we were scheduled to canvass in Walker, Iowa, a place neither of us knew much about. We did know it was rural, agricultural and a fifteen-minute highway drive away. In other words, we were heading into the heart of Republican country

We were there: Walker, Iowa – population 775. Almost as if time had stood still, Walker could have easily been standing in the middle of the previous century: big frame houses, long front yards and brick storefronts. Everything was plain, neat, simple. No big SUVs or stylish cars, just pickup trucks and men in blue jeans, work boots and unzipped ski jackets over flannel shirts. One business, a tavern on the corner, was named Corner Tavern. At the end of the road on another street called Mill Street – an actual grain mill. Plain, neat, simple.

It was cold and snowy, and most walks had not been shoveled. We knocked on the doors of the addresses on our list. People either weren't home or didn't bother to answer their doors. We approached one house and made it as far as the porch before an irritated old man opened his door, yelling, "Get off of my property!" Two Irish Setters with floppy ears and shiny, long hair bolted out. My family's first dog was an Irish Setter named Rags. She had been gentle and friendly, just as these dogs seemed to be. But Bob and I were strangers, and even friendly dogs have teeth that bite. We got out of there as quickly as we could, turning and running, practically falling down the porch steps. We ran without looking back, across the shin-deep snow in the front yard and back to Bob's van.

Once we were safely inside his van, we looked at each other and began laughing. Not a tickled laugh, but a nervous one. The kind that starts off small and builds to a crescendo, then suddenly stops with a sort of sadness that is sometimes punctuated with tears. We didn't cry. We just sat in shock at the fact that someone had actually sicced his dogs on us.

"Can you believe that crap!" Bob shouted.

He asked the question rhetorically. I didn't answer him. I didn't need to. We both knew it was a pretty screwed-up thing for anyone to do, even for a Republican.

He cranked up his van and shifted into reverse. We shook off what had just happened and headed out to the next cluster of houses on our lists. We drove and canvassed until night fell, riding along the long, dark, winding highways dotted with deer and wild rabbits. We drove until Walker got smaller and smaller in his rearview mirror.

We'd hit fifty-two homes. We didn't get any supporter cards signed, but we didn't get killed, either. In fact, we were proud of the work done and gave each other a big hug before going our separate ways. I was tired and could feel a cold coming on, and somehow could also sense that I would be dreaming about Rags that night.

৵

By week's end a pattern had set in: up at dawn, canvass for four hours in the morning, take a break, eat, canvass for four hours in the evening, go back to the hotel, pass out from exhaustion. And even though the routine was the same, the communities we canvassed were becoming wildly different. Thus far, I had canvassed in rural farm communities like Walker and suburban, middle-class communities like Marion. By the fourth day of the get-out-the-vote campaign, I was on the trail in Cedar Rapids proper – from the affluent to inner-city foster homes.

The day spent in an affluent community started out at the "station house" of Dave and Lisa, both optometrists. Their home was gorgeous: large, blond brick, sprawling yards. A black baby grand piano stood to the right as one entered. Italian marble tile in the foyer intersected hardwood floors throughout, including in the full gym in the basement, complete with basketball hoops. Lisa had a nice spread of coffee, tea, muffins, and hot cinnamon rolls with melting icing set out for us. I got paired with Jack from Evanston, Illinois. We canvassed Dave and Lisa's neighborhood. Each home we approached was as beautiful as the one before it. We parked the car at one end of the block and walked up one side and down the other. Jack, previously a news reporter, knocked on doors and talked to the people as I completed canvass sheets and filled out supporter cards. He had gone to college in Iowa in the '70s and had caucused before, so he was easy and natural as he engaged them in conversation. The people were friendly. They asked intelligent questions. They had a grasp of the issues, and they were definitely decided. Overwhelmingly they were supporting Obama.

At the end of our four-hour shifts, all of the canvassers met back at Dave and Lisa's. Jack and I had hit forty-three homes and got three supporter cards. Lisa had another spread laid out. This time there were platters of deli meats, lettuce, tomatoes, pickles, condiments, chips and Pellegrino sparkling mineral water. We sat and ate, laughing and sharing success stories. The sun reflected off the snow outside, piercing through the dining room windows, reflecting our happy spirits of a good, easy day's work.

୬

The next day was spent in the inner city. I teamed up with Marla and Ann Marie, a middle-aged white couple with three adopted Korean kids. They picked me up and, as usual, were bickering and talking at the same time, then asking each other, "Whaddya say?" They were as funny as any other married couple that had been together for a very long time. The kids were in the back seats of the mini-van watching videos. Marla, Ann Marie and I were all coughing, popping cough drops and drinking bottled water. The sun was high, the temperature in the mid-20s. Sidewalks were slick and snow-covered. Our spirits were high, and there was adventure in our hearts. We were city girls headed into Cedar Rapids' inner city.

We had sheets and sheets of apartments to canvass, over one hundred addresses total. The canvass started with a lot of "not homes."

It was Sunday, so people were either at church or getting ready for the afternoon football games. We started catching people at home. By the third complex, we encountered Larry. He answered the door wearing a baseball cap and underpants – dirty, yellowed underpants. Ann Marie let out a gasp at the shocking sight of the potbellied, flabby, nearly naked man. She regrouped and went into her script about the caucus. The guy across the hall, whom I was talking to, wasn't sure if he was going to caucus or not. Larry said he was going to caucus and would caucus for Obama. Ann Marie gave him a supporter card to complete. He stepped inside and returned with a pair of jeans on, and some homemade sausage made of deer meat, cheese and jalapeño peppers. He offered the roll of sausage to his neighbor across the hall, and then gave us the thumbs-up and a scattered-tooth smile. Once inside the van, we took turns rapidly telling the whole man-with-the-dingy-yellow/gray-two-week-old-looking-crusty-crotch-funky-cotton-drawers story to Marla. We laughed and made every kind of "nasty man" joke possible, all the way to the next complex.

The next address on our list turned out to be a group home for foster kids who were turning 18 and maxing out of the system. We had the names of eleven teens that were planning to caucus for Obama. We met with the social worker, and he assured us that the kids would be there. They were planning on making it a field trip activity. One hitch: the agency couldn't use its vans to take the kids to a political event. We told them not to worry, that we'd have enough cars there to take a group of kids in each car. Another hitch: the agency also could not take the teens out in separate groups. The teens and chaperones had to always be together. We thought for a moment and said, "No problem."

We remembered Beth and Zett from Chicago, and that their mini-bus sat twelve or thirteen. We told the social worker that we'd have a mini-bus there to pick everyone up. We had no idea whether that was totally true or not. The teens were jumping up and down and high-fiving. The social worker smiled and thanked us. We had no idea whether or not Zett had scheduled his mini-bus for the same time to pick up other supporters. We quietly, collectively decided that we'd worry about this small detail later. Right now, we were getting signatures on supporter cards and just praying that it would all work out. During the flurry of activity and signatures, we even got one more kid to sign up. Twelve supporter cards! What a coup!

The next complex was another hit. We walked away with four supporter cards. A twenty-something black woman named Tarika hobbled to the door on a swollen and bandaged leg, saw us ablaze in Obama gear and looked as if she would cry from excitement. She otherwise looked haggard and a bit frazzled. She had two sons. One was an infant cooing, kicking and air-boxing as he lay on a lumpy, floral couch; the other was a toddler, close by her side peeking out from behind her hips. Tarika invited us in and asked us to have a seat. Our campaign training, for safety reasons, was to remain outside and in the open; however, it was cold, and the woman couldn't stand in the doorway on that busted leg. Besides, among the toy-cluttered floor, chairs and tables, there wasn't anyplace to sit, so we respectfully stepped inside and stood as we began talking about the upcoming caucus. She listened intently, occasionally biting her lip and rubbing her leg.

We finished our spiel on Obama's stand on the issues and ended with asking her, "So, will you caucus for Obama on January 3rd?"

She started talking, hesitated, and got choked up. She said she had gotten calls from other campaigns and had gotten their literature, but was disappointed that the only African American candidate in the race hadn't reached out to her – another African American. She said she had never caucused before and with that banged-up leg (the result of some fuss, tussle and disagreement with her boyfriend/children's father) wasn't sure if she could stand that long. In the end, though, she decided that for Obama she'd do whatever it took to help get him elected. We thanked her and assured her that if need be we'd make sure someone from the campaign would be with her every literal step of the way, babysitting her children, offering her a shoulder to lean on, or a folding chair to sit in.

This time we knew we could make good on our promises. I had signed up to be an on-site sitter for "Obama babies," and with this being

Ann Marie's assigned precinct, she would be taking personal responsibility for getting this young woman to the caucus site. We hugged and laughed, and waved good-bye to the boys. Tarika said that we had made her day. From the look of pride and broad smile on her otherwise burdened and forlorn face, we believed her. What she didn't know and probably couldn't fully grasp was that she had made ours as well.

While Ann Marie and I were talking to Tarika, Marla had her hands full downstairs on the second floor with another black family, the Bozemans, comprising a mother and three children between the ages of 18 and early 20s. By the time we caught up with Marla, the Bozemans were explaining (rather loudly) that they were Hillary Clinton supporters because it was "time for a woman to be in charge!"

"Forget 'bout Obama being a black man," the oldest child continued on. "What have black men done for us? Nothing! It's time for women to rule, baby!"

Well, Ann Marie stepped in, using all of her lawyer skills to compare and contrast the two candidates' stands on issues. When we finally left, we had three Obama supporter cards in hand – one each from the mother, the 18-year-old boy and his 19-year-old sister. The oldest sister was still supporting Hillary, "because it was time for women to rule!"

I couldn't have disagreed with her more, nor could I begrudge her feelings. I didn't express or try to reveal mine. I didn't know what her experience with black, or any other, men had been. We were just happy to have the additional supporter cards and left the Bozemans, including the young sista' with the men demons, before they either changed their minds or something more interesting ensued.

In the last apartment building we canvassed, Ann Marie converted a Bill Richardson supporter and got him to sign an Obama supporter card. Obama's anti-Iraq War stance was what finally won him over. The rest of the apartments were either "not homes" or outright no answers. Marla lucked out and talked to a guy whose place looked like it belonged to the flesh-eating serial killer Jeffrey Dahmer: black furniture, black walls, no lights, creepy.

He invited her inside. "No thanks!" she screamed, backing away and getting the hell out of there – quick. We crossed him off the list and checked the "wrong address" box.

We looked back on our day. We'd knocked on sixty-four doors and turned in a handsome load of supporter cards – nineteen in all! Our day in "the hood" had been fun, adventurous, and very successful.

THE GROUND GAME

I'd been canvassing in Iowa for almost one week before I fully understood the strategy on the ground. I only knew that seemingly we were ringing the same doorbells again and again, and I'd begun to wonder, *What in the hell are we doing out here?* I finally asked Doug, the intern who was staying with Dave and Lisa. He broke it down for me.

"Well, Michelle, we want to touch some voters three times before the caucus. And we want to touch some of 'em six times," he explained.

"How do we know which is which and who is who?"

"Oh, we've got the stats on which precincts turn out heavy and which ones are light. Plus we've got the market studies on who's spending money on what kinds of stuff: what magazines, what shoes, what foods, what entertainment. You know, stuff like that. Based on that kind of information, we know which areas are more likely Democratic, so we can go light there. You know, maintain the base. But the areas that are Republican, likely Republican or swing both ways, well, we press hard in those."

"Yeah, but stats and figures and magazine subscriptions only tell you so much," I rebutted. "You still need a big field operation on the ground, like the old-style machine politics that we used to have in Chicago. You know at the precinct, ward, and aldermanic levels."

"You're right," Doug said. "That's why I'm here. I'm actually from Texas, you know, going to the University of Texas, studying political science. I've been out here for the last six months, living with Dave and Lisa. I'm part of the community. Gettin' to know the people. Talkin' to 'em. Gettin' them little by little, to sign up to be supporters, precinct captains, station house hosts, caucus-goers, whatever."

"Oh," I said. "Cool. Real cool."

And the light bulb went on. That was the game. It was long-term strategic planning that had been in place from the very start of the campaign.

I listened and thought about what Doug was telling me. I started remembering episodic events and began connecting the dots. I remembered the young high school kid in Atlanta who was the precinct captain of his school. That was back in February of 2007! I also remembered the different groups at the Chicago headquarters saying good-bye to co-workers who were being shipped off to Des Moines, Dubuque, Iowa City, Cedar Rapids and other cities of Iowa. I remembered and could picture the small going-away parties. That had been back in May, June and July of 2007, more than six months ago.

The picture of the ground game was becoming clearer. Just as Doug had described it, Obama campaign staff from other cities and states across the country were deployed to Iowa long before the Clinton, Edwards or Richardson campaigns even thought about doing so. Staff moved in and settled into neighborhoods. In the precincts that voted heavily Republican or leaning Republican, more than one staffer was deployed. And once they were in place, they joined the churches. They shopped in the neighborhood grocery stores and gassed up at local stations. They ate at ma-and-pa diners. They went to PTA meetings and high school sporting events. And at each stop along the way, they'd talk to people. But mostly, they'd listen, waiting to hear the one thought or concern or utterance or sentence that indicated that this person could become an Obama supporter. For some, it was his stance against "the silly war" in Iraq; for others, it was his support of women and family issues; and yet for others it was the fact that he was a fresh face and new voice that talked about changing the stale and stagnant politics of Washington, D. C. The ground game was operating at this nuanced of a level: talking, listening, waiting, persuading, patience.

And as the campaign workers talked about Obama, people listened and opened up and talked back. The people of Iowa weren't talking to strangers, but rather to people they'd seen in church or at the store or at school meetings. Trust was built, and confidence in Obama was growing.

The pre-caucus ground game was slow, methodical, expensive. It took patience and resolve. It also took resources, both human and financial. The strategy was brilliant, and as old as Abe Lincoln. During the 1840 presidential campaign, Abraham Lincoln (then a member of the Whig Party) described a similar plan to his county committee members: "Our intention is to so organize the whole State so that every Whig can be brought to the polls. . . . Divide your county into small districts and appoint in each a sub-committee, whose duty shall be to make a perfect list of all voters . . . and ascertain with certainty for whom they will vote. . . . Keep a constant watch on the doubtful voters and . . . have them talked to by those in whom they have the most confidence. . . . On election day, see every Whig is brought to the polls."[12]

So, when Doug talked about "touching" a voter three times or six times, he was really talking about implementing a tried-and-true strategy from over one hundred and sixty years ago. The modern-day version of Lincoln's strategy looked as follows:

Market researchers looked at the demographics of a particular community and began to build a profile of that community. They were hired to find out what are the habits of the people in this community, so that social and political assumptions could be reasonably made. For instance, people who buy organic foods, drive economy cars, wear sensible, foot-saving shoes, and subscribe to *Hiking Magazine* are more inclined to vote for a candidate, like Obama, who is athletic, healthy, concerned with the environment and preservation of the nation's natural resources.

The goal is to sort out the staunch Democrats and Republicans from the Independent swing voters as well as the elusive undecided voters.

The lifelong Democratic voters would be touched three times: an initial contact to make sure he or she was going to vote and to get a commitment of some sort – to canvass; to donate; to become a precinct

---

[12] Theis, Paul A. and William P. Stoponkus, All About Politics: Questions and Answers on the U. S. Political Process, New York: Bowker, 1972, p.13.

worker or captain; to caucus for Obama. If those voters were support-ing Obama, we'd thank them and come back later (the second "touch") to invite them to a rally or event. If the Democratic voters were support-ing another candidate, we'd turn the name over to a higher-up, like Doug, who'd call on them later and try to persuade them to leave the Clinton, Edwards, or Richardson team and to join ours. Once the Democratic voters who were supporting Obama were established, we'd contact them for a third time on the morning of caucus day.

The staunch Republican voters were simpler. No means no. In some cases, no meant hell no! We'd contact them once, mark our sheets to indicate their intentions and not contact them again.

This flushing out process allowed us to concentrate our efforts on the "likely," "leaning," and "undecided" voters. These were the meat of the voting pool, and the people who had to be persuaded to vote for Obama. These were the people we'd "touch" or contact the most: initially to find out their voting intentions; a second time to explain is-sues, answer questions, invite them to a rally; a third time to answer more questions and to ask them to caucus; a fourth time to remind them to caucus and answer any caucus procedural questions; a fifth time to place door-hangers with caucus times and addresses on them; and a final time on caucus day to see if they needed any assistance getting to the caucus.

As part of the ground game, people like me came in to do the door-knocking, question answering, cajoling, persuading, convincing; the force to get the people to the polls on January 3rd to caucus for Obama. It was a mighty task, and by the time the ground game got around to our part, over 900 people from across the country had flown, driven and moved in to fulfill our promise to get out the vote.[13]

☙

---

[13] During the December 16, 2008, conference call between Samir Randolph, of the Iowa State campaign staff, and the "Iowa City/Cedar Rapids Obama Volunteers" it was explained that over 2,000 volunteers from California to the East Coast wanted to canvass in Iowa. The Iowa State campaign office decided that they could not handle the training and accommodations for that many people, so the number of volunteers accepted to participate was cut down to 900.

It was New Year's Eve, and I was missing my friends and family and James something terrible. I was even going to miss my best friend Denise's marriage celebration. This was her first time getting married, and I should have been there. I had no way, however, of keeping my nine-day canvassing commitment to the campaign and of attending her happy moment in Chicago, too. The best I could do was to phone in to the celebration at an appointed time to wish Denise and Michael Edwards my best, via speaker phone. So at 8:30 that evening, I called their house to take part in the toasts that our friends were giving. Our other friend Mickey was emceeing the program, and things were running pretty smoothly.

I came across the line, yelling out to the crowd, "Can y'all hear me?"

"Yeah!" they responded.

I began an upbeat riff about marriage and old age and love and stinky feet. Despite the tears forming at the base of my throat, I gave the toast without my voice giving way. I ended it with tying her marriage to the campaign going on by saying, "And although you're now an Edwards, I hope that you're still supporting Obama."

Denise, Mike and the crowd burst into laughter at my clever pun on the surname Edwards, given that at the time John Edwards was proving to be a formidable candidate against Obama. After the toast, Mickey presented them with a bottle of Dom Perignon champagne that I'd bought – a part guilty, part I'm-so-happy-for-you gift. Mickey and her husband Odell bought them a pair of Waterford crystal champagne flutes to compliment my gift. Denise was happy. She even said she was going to cry (something rarely done). That made me happy, knowing that my very best friend was pleased, and that I had shared in the sweetness of her moment.

I hung up and turned my attention to the tables filled with the Obama family of volunteers who'd gathered at the Irish Democrat restaurant. Across the way were Hillary and Biden supporters. Around the corner at another table were more Obama supporters, including Michelle Obama's aunt and uncle from Chicago. The place was loud with laughter and conversation. Two couples were shooting pool in the back of the

room. Three large-screen televisions were on the sports channels air-
ing various football games. The scents of hamburgers, nachos, buffalo
wings and beer clung to the air. The atmosphere was vibrant, electric, the
stroke of midnight just a few hours away.

We left the restaurant and drove a short distance to the Cedar Rapids campaign office. A statewide call-in with the Iowa state campaign
coordinators was scheduled for shortly after midnight. At the stroke of
twelve, we popped the champagne corks off bottles of Cook's champagne and blew our noisemakers. Everyone was hugging and wishing
each other a Happy New Year. I hugged and kissed cheeks and sipped
cheap champagne as I watched the people who filled the campaign office. We'd come from everywhere: Chicago; Austin, Texas; University of
California at Berkeley; Indianapolis; Evanston, Illinois; the south suburbs of Chicago; from every corner of the country. There were young
people and old ones – one volunteer was 82 years old. There were blacks
and whites, and people with disabilities; a young white guy with a mental
disability stood alongside an older brother with a hearing and speech
impairment.

I sipped some more wine and thought about Mike and Denise. I
wished they were here, and I wished I was there. I was bringing in a new
year away from home, away from my mother, away from my best friend
and the rest of my friends, away from James. I thought about him and
wondered how he was ringing in the New Year. I tried texting. It didn't
work – signal busy. It was New Year's Eve after all, and folks across the
nation were sharing "I love you's" and "Happy New Year!" sentiments.

A loud crackle from the telephones filled the room. The Iowa state
coordinator's voice was coming through the speakers. He congratulated
us on our hard work and then began running down the numbers. Across
the state, collectively we had knocked on over 40,000 doors and made
over 16,000 contacts on this one day alone. On average, during that week
of Get Out the Caucus, we were knocking on over 55,000 doors a day!

The room burst into a frenzy of hoots and hollers at the news of
the big numbers. We knew the numbers were true. We felt them, in our
aching legs and thighs and stiff bones; in our tired feet and backs; in our

chapped lips and aching hands; in the missing of our families. The news was good, and it was our moment to exhale. So we did. We hooted and hollered and smiled outwardly, and beamed inwardly. We took pride in the power of what determination and unity together could do. I couldn't be sure, but I thought, *We just might be able to win this thing!* The only something I was certain of, I was a part of something big that was growing, of something seemingly unstoppable!

༄

There were two days left before caucus day, and a lot of ground had been covered. There were voters who needed to be "touched" two more times, and there were voters we'd been unable to thus far catch at home. So, back to the streets. Because it was New Year's Day, we only canvassed for four hours, during the afternoon shift.

We were canvassing in Walker, Iowa again. I was paired with a young lady named Amber. She was a local who had never canvassed before. I gave her a crash course in canvassing, and she gave me confidence in hitting this rather unfriendly, Republican territory. She knew a lot of the people on our lists, even attended church with some. She was familiar with how the town was laid out and where the addresses were. She shared that she was a lifelong Republican who was crossing over because Obama had opposed the war from the beginning. That made me instantly reflect on the *Des Moines Register* poll that predicted Obama the Democratic winner by a 7% lead, based in large part on high turnout of young voters, first-time voters and crossover Republicans.[14]

I smiled.

With the winter sun in our faces, we began the fifteen-minute drive to Walker. We smiled at each other and began chatting about life: work and kids; husbands and the price of gasoline; deer hunting and food shopping; recipes for making good chicken soup. Through slight drifts

---

[14] In Thomas Beaumont's "New Iowa Poll: Obama Widens Lead Over Clinton," *Des Moines Register,* January 1, 2008, he reported on a telephone survey taken December 27-30, 2007 of 800 likely Democratic caucus-goers. The survey showed that 32 percent supported Obama versus 25 percent for Clinton and 24 percent for Edwards; and among non-Democratic supporters, 40 percent described themselves as independent and another 5 percent as Republicans.

of snow and soothing sunshine, we drove on to begin our four hours of canvassing in the countryside.

The strategy for this canvass was to contact the same people we had contacted four days earlier. On the first trip we had knocked on doors, talked to supporters and given them literature on how to canvass as well as flyers about the upcoming rally. This go round, we had full-color door hangers with Barack's picture, the caucus date and specific caucus locations printed on them. We hit all of the addresses on our lists. Most folks either weren't home, or simply not answering. Those who did were avid supporters, many of whom were Independents and Republicans – including Mary, a feisty 92-year-old who promised to caucus for Obama. At the end of the canvass, Amber and I had done well, including getting three supporter cards. By five that evening all of the canvassers headed home to rest and enjoy what was left of New Year's Day 2008.

The following afternoon, a major rally was being held in Cedar Rapids. We were scheduled to canvass in the morning, attend the rally in the afternoon, and canvass again in the evening.

The convention hall in downtown Cedar Rapids was already buzzing with nearly one hundred volunteers when Doug and I arrived about an hour before the event was to begin. The energy was high, and rising, as people began seeing other people they knew. I saw a small contingency of women from South Suburban Women for Obama. We hugged and greeted each other and talked about how exciting it was to be a part of this whole process. Within the next half hour, nearly five hundred people had arrived and were filling the seats. The disc jockey was playing the soul-rocking sounds of Aretha Franklin's "Respect," The Staple Singers' "I'll Take You There," and the mellow voice of Curtis Mayfield. People continued to pour in. The seats were now full. Folks were starting to stand, filling in the floor space. By the time Senator Obama took to the stage, over a thousand people were there – all cheering, clapping and chanting, "O–Bama! '08! O–Bama! '08!"

The senator was sensational and on message. He talked about hope and unity and a new day for America; about ending the Iraq War and easing the burdens of middle-class America; about engaging everyday Americans in the process of governing; and about restoring our good name in the international world. The crowd responded with cheers and picture-taking. The press corps, from around the world, worked the crowd: taking pictures of children sitting high atop the shoulders of their dads; talking to seniors in the reserved-seating area; or interviewing people the most decked out in Obama gear. The room was electric.

We didn't have long to bask in the excitement before it was back to work. We were grouped into teams to hit the streets again to knock on doors and hand out door-hangers. I was paired with Jack from Evanston again. He was traveling with his close friend Shelton (an investment and insurance fraud attorney) and David Orr (the seven-day interim mayor of Chicago after Mayor Harold Washington died).[15] All four of us piled into Shelton's car, canvass sheets in hand, ready to begin our respective routes. Because there were four of us and two areas to hit, David and Shelton took the car to drive the trailer park community. Jack and I were "walkers," which meant we got dropped off and walked. We had forty-plus homes to hit – not bad had the weather been warmer. The temperature was 2 degrees, the wind chill below zero. It hit me as soon as I left the warmth of the car. I knew this was going to be a hard canvass and a long two hours. The cold was bad enough, but the darkness was a challenge too. Folks in Iowa are pretty practical and don't leave their porch lights burning unnecessarily, so reading addresses was nearly impossible – especially since my glasses kept fogging as the steam rose through my scarf that covered my nose.

Oh Lord, I prayed more than once. *I hope I can make it.*

We started at one end of a long, winding street and worked our way through a few of our sheets. I'd taken the scarf off my nose so that my glasses wouldn't fog, but my lips began to tighten and hurt as the frigid wind hit my face. We kept knocking and walking, talking to potential voters and leaving door-hangers. I searched my bag for a lip balm and

---

[15] Chicago Mourns Mayor Washington, Council Picks New Mayor Next Week," *Chicago Tribune*: 1, 1987-11-27. After Harold Washington's death, as vice-mayor, David Orr served as interim mayor from November 25, 1987 to December 2, 1987, when Eugene Sawyer was elected mayor of Chicago by the City Council.

hand warmer packs. My fingers were aching, and bending them was becoming difficult. I could barely hold on to my canvass sheets and kept dropping them each time I tried to check the appropriate boxes.

We finally reached a home where a woman actually let us in out of the cold. As Jack talked to her, I took the opportunity to fish out the hand warmers, blow my nose and apply some more lip balm. I begin to feel better, though my fingers were beginning to sting. I didn't want to leave the warmth of the house, but the time had come for us to move on. We got outside and rounded the corner to hit the next street. We had three long streets, probably the equivalent of a couple of miles. We'd covered about half of that, maybe twenty-plus homes, before I couldn't go on any more. My fingers were aching. My toes were aching. My cheeks and nose were aching. I couldn't write or even hold onto the sheets or door-hangers because my fingers had become too stiff to grip them. After dropping them, for the last time, I told Jack that I was calling Doug to come pick us up.

"I'm sorry," I said. "I can't stay out in this weather."

He looked at me with a sympathetic eye and agreed that that was a good idea. Jack and I both were from Chicago. We'd both lived through treacherous winters. We knew what being exposed to below-zero winds for too long could do to the body. I was afraid of getting frostbite and didn't want to risk it. Jack didn't look too good either. His cheeks and ears were a deep red, and his hands were an ashy white. We must have looked a sight standing on a person's doorstep. I loved Barack and wanted him to win Iowa. I wasn't willing to lose a baby finger or toe for the cause, though.

Doug got to where we were in no time at all, and to my surprise, Jack wanted to stay out there and finish the route. He'd have to do about twenty more homes in the dark, in the cold, by himself. For a moment I felt a pang of guilt for quitting, but as another biting wind whipped across my face, I quickly said, "Okay then. I'll see you back at Dave and Lisa's place."

I didn't know that Doug had told Jack that he'd drop me off; give me a crash course on entering the data that he was working, which would allow me to finish up his work in the warmth of a home; and then Doug would drive back to Jack and finish the route. When Doug explained the switch-off, I felt better. I settled back in the front seat of the car. The heat blowing onto my boots and face felt wonderful. I couldn't wait to get back to Dave and Lisa's. I was cold and hungry. I folded my arms underneath my breasts, leaned my head back and closed my eyes, letting the warmth of the manufactured car heat take my mind off of my aching body and empty stomach.

The aroma of pot roast hit me as we entered the house. It reminded me of home. I hadn't had a hot, home-cooked meal since I'd left Chicago, just sandwiches and chips, sardines and Ritz crackers, beanie-weenies and bottled water. My mouth watered. My home-training, however, made me say, "Oh, no thank you" when Lisa offered me some dinner. Doug quickly ran through how to enter the data onto the Excel spreadsheet and left to join Jack. There weren't many sheets to enter, so I finished up pretty quickly. And just as I did, Lisa insisted that I join them for dinner. Manners aside, I was hungry and tired, so I thanked her and said yes. She'd prepared a large spread: pot roast and carrots, baked potatoes, string beans, tossed salad, Pellegrino water and red wine. I passed on the wine and savored everything else. Lisa was an excellent cook and enjoyed watching people enjoy her food. About halfway through my meal, Shelton and David returned from their route at the trailer park. They were hungry as well. Lisa dished up two plates as they removed their coats and boots and began washing their hands. We started sharing stories about the people we'd met out on the canvass trail.

Shelton and David started their meals with the wine, so the conversation quickly became lively and humorous. Shortly thereafter, Jack and Doug came in. They removed their coats and boots and joined us for dinner. Although Lisa had prepared enough food for a small army, she put a few chicken breasts in the oven for safe measure. By the time she served coffee and coffeecake for dessert, the men were on their second bottle of wine and we were all laughing and sharing stories. Now, you can't get that many Chicagoans together and not talk politics; and you can't talk Chicago politics without talking about Harold Washington, the first black mayor; and you can't talk about Harold Washington without talking about the tumultuous situation that ensued after his death.

We all sat enthralled at the words coming from David Orr's mouth, a first-hand retelling of what those seven days had been like for him as mayor after Harold Washington's death from a heart attack. He talked about the battle between the old guard who wanted Eugene Sawyer in as mayor and the change agents of Harold Washington's guard, who wanted Timothy Evans as mayor; and about how he had to both calm the city and bring both sides to the table. In the end, the old establishment won out, although David had actually wanted Timothy Evans to win. I leaned back from the conversation and took a deep breath. He'd just taken me down a late eighties memory lane. I remembered that time. Chicago was a city in shock at the death of its mayor, and reacted with anger. People were angry because Mayor Washington had suddenly died and their second-term elected leader was gone forever. Other people were angry because they believed he'd been murdered, poisoned to induce or mimic a heart attack. And still others were angry at people for believing such a theory. I remembered the anger and Interim Mayor Orr's reaction to it. He fought fire with calm and resolve as he played referee to the two warring factions: the old guard of mainly white, conservative aldermen versus the new guard of blacks and progressives. During that time, he didn't reveal who he was supporting and stayed focused on trying to keep the citizens of Chicago assured that whoever won, the process itself would have been legal and aboveboard. His task and the times were not easy.

I could hardly believe that here I, on faculty at the college that bore the name of the late, great Harold Washington, sat at the table with doctors and attorneys and a former mayor – sitting in our stocking feet talking politics and history, breaking bread and drinking wine together. That space between nostalgia and reality was both superb and surreal. I wanted to take a picture of it, but chose to just capture the image in my memory. It would be one that I'd never forget. Here we were, Barack's little army, tired but happy and looking forward to the next day – the Iowa caucus.

CAUCUS DAY

Tired as I was the night before, I could hardly sleep. This was the day we'd all waited for. This is why we had traveled from near and far to be in Iowa. My clock was set for 6 a.m., but I was already awake. The talking heads on "Morning Joe" were predicting a tight, three-way race on the Democratic side – between Obama, Clinton and Edwards. Although I'd been on the ground for eight days knocking on God only knows how many doors, and despite what the polls were showing, I still didn't have a definitive feel for who would win. Iowans can be pretty close-mouthed about their political preferences, so the candidate I'd most heard they'd vote for was "Undecided." I agreed with the talking heads – it was going to be a tight race.

I grabbed the day's edition of the *Des Moines Register* and *The Gazette*, a local paper. Political coverage was splattered across both. The presidential contest was on the minds of nearly everybody. I was feeling good. The weather was nice – a balmy upper 20s. The sun was out. Politics were in the air. This was the last day for knocking on doors before the people of Iowa would caucus at 7 o'clock that night. I prayed that all of our hard work would pay off. I prayed that we'd make history by electing Obama the winner of the Democratic caucus. Doug picked me up and I sat shotgun, letting the sun warm my face. Looking out over the snowy landscape, I silently prayed.

We got to Carol and Elden's in Marion, and Jeff was already commanding the troops. He explained the strategy for the day. Today we were only knocking on the 1Ls, 2Ls and 3Ls – in other words, the people who were "definitely" going to caucus for Obama (1Ls and 2Ls) or were leaning that way (3Ls). I was paired with Lauren, an attorney and former state representative who had worked in the Illinois Legislature with Obama. She was a talker – either to me or to someone on her car speaker phone, or to whomever answered the door when we knocked. She was fun, and the route was light. We were getting a lot of people who were not home, and the few who were there were either sick (like the young man on crutches) or "severely sick," as an elderly woman explained her husband's condition; one woman was in the hospital because she was about to have her baby "at any time now," as the expectant grandfather explained. All legitimate reasons as to why they wouldn't be caucusing tonight, all good reasons for us to begin to worry.

These were the people we were counting on, who had indicated that they would definitely be there, but as life would have it, they couldn't and therefore wouldn't. Lauren and I began to have a mood swing. This was the one thing we'd feared – a low turnout. We were nearing the end of our list and got a "yes, I'll be there" response and "yes, you can put a yard sign out front." We felt a little better after putting out a few yard signs and finishing our first list. We took an unofficial break before starting the second packet, and stopped in a Mexican restaurant with an Irish name. The truth is, we needed to escape the campaign for a while and just "girl talk." We laughed and talked about which parts of our bodies bloated during various times of the month; hot flashes; night sweats; husbands; kids, and the best thrift store shopping around Chicago. As much fun as that was, it was time to get back to work. And we both hoped that the second half would be more successful that the first. It was!

The first few doors that we knocked on, the people were home and giving us the thumbs-up sign. These were the young housewives who were now home after doing their morning chores, or college kids with a half-day schedule, and high school seniors who didn't have an after-school job to rush off to. In short, these were the young voters, the new voters, the first-timers, the base that the Obama campaign was counting on. By the time we finished our second packet, we had way more yeses than no's, and we felt really good.

Although we were an hour behind our scheduled return time, we entered the station house boldly and loudly, giving Jeff the good news about our canvass. Jeff, a very quiet, steady, low-key young man, was an organizer and labor attorney. He was impartial to our excitement and gave no indication of what the predicted voter turnout would be. He just smiled pleasantly, said, "That's good, that's great," and proceeded to give us our caucus assignments.

I was assigned to the Marion City Hall caucus in Marion, Iowa. I got paired with Mark, who was scheduled to pick up and drop off a senior citizen who'd be caucusing at that location. I had the job of watching the "Obama babies." Meaning, anyone caucusing for Obama who had young children that needed watching while they did so could leave them with me. I sort of had a problem with watching other folks' kids as if I was some sort a mammy or nanny, but I reminded myself that this cause was bigger than me and my pride. If this was the role that the campaign needed me to play so that the parents could vote, I was willing to do it.

We arrived at the Marion City Hall, a small, quaint, two-story structure, and walked Norma (the elderly black woman we picked up) over to the community assembly room where the caucus was to take place. I remembered that we (the out-of-towners) had been instructed not to go inside the caucus, to be low-profile, and definitely not to vote! I decided to set up my "Obama babies" corner out in the lobby where there was a table and a few chairs. I ended up with four children gathered around me, ranging in age from 4 to 6 to about 10 and 11. I sat out mini granola bars and a small carton of milk. The oldest kid with me was playing on his Game Boy, quite oblivious to the history that was in the making. The younger children drew pictures on scratch paper. I was hunched over Christopher, the 6-year-old, admiring his drawing of a bunny rabbit, when all of a sudden a large group of people led by the Obama precinct captain came out of the assembly room and headed straight towards me.

Uh-oh! What's happening? Have I done something? I nervously thought. Although we'd been trained in a mock caucus, this was my first live one, and I didn't totally know what to expect or what was going on.

JoAnn, the precinct captain, quickly explained that the assembly room regularly used for council meetings, community meetings and caucuses was too small. She explained that they were setting up the Obama and Edwards people out in the lobby, as she tacked up "Stand With Obama" and "Stand For Unity" signs on a column near me and the children. I asked if she needed me to move, and she responded, "Oh no, sweetie, you and the kids stay right here."

The Edwards precinct captain drug a six-foot table out from somewhere to separate the two camps. Here I was smack dab in the center of the caucus, both ironic and exciting. Maybe it was because I'd followed the rules that I was now being rewarded with a ringside seat to history. Maybe it was fate and I was just where I was supposed to be. No matter. I was there, right in the middle of a live caucus!

People began pouring out of the small community assembly room and kept coming through the front doors, and from the parking lots, and seemingly from out of nowhere and everywhere all at once. The Obama people lined up on one side of the lobby to my right, and the Edwards people on my left. The lobby began to swell with people as they "stood" literally and figuratively to caucus for their candidates of choice. At promptly 7 p.m., the city hall doors were closed. The first count began. This count was done to determine which of the candidates had enough votes to be viable and remain in the race. Each group – Clinton and Biden (both inside the assembly room); Obama and Edwards (both in the lobby); and the Richardson, Dodd and Kucinich groups (on the staircase) began counting off the number of people in their respective groups. The total number of people packed into the small-town city hall was 342. While not a large number, it was quite significant. Only 147 people had turned out to caucus four years earlier. The excitement was building. Even the children seemed to be caught up in the moment of history and required minimal watching.

The second count was about to begin. I couldn't hear how many people were caucusing for Hillary Clinton or Joe Biden, because there were no microphones or bullhorns in the assembly hall. Many of the people in the lobby looked a bit confused and anxious. Small conversations sprouted throughout the crowds, many of them asking what was going on. JoAnn had been moving back and forth between the lobby and assembly hall. She came back to the lobby and loudly asked that each person count off the next number as she pointed to that person. She asked everyone with a "red x" marked on their hands to raise their hands, and as she counted them off to lower their hands. A tremendous hush blanketed the lobby as the counting began and the anticipation mounted. My heart was racing. The Obama crowd looked much bigger than the Edwards crowd, but I couldn't really gauge or guess by how much.

The counting continued – "53, 54, 55."

The excitement was mounting.

"61, 62, 63."

Only half the Obama folks had counted off. The wave of hands lowering continued. I did a quick calculation of those counted compared to those left to be counted and quickly surmised that Obama had well over 100 people, nearly a third of the total people there. *He will definitely get some of the nine delegates at stake*, I thought. *Doggone it, he might even win this thing!*

"101,102, 103!"

People not only had their hands raised high, but their chests were stuck out, and that determined look of pride that washes over you when you realize that you're part of something big, momentous, historical. I, too, was proud to be there. I saw a couple of camera flashes go off and decided to sneak in a few pictures of the moment myself. I turned away from the kids long enough to snap two pictures and catch the tail end of the count.

"141, 142, 143!"

Obama folks totaled nearly half of the people there and more than all of the entire total of the previous presidential caucus. The Obama caucuses erupted into shouts and high-fives as everyone began to suddenly realize that we seemed to be heading towards winning. The Edwards folks still had to be counted, and I didn't know the total for Hillary. No matter, we all could feel what was happening. It was in the air. It was in the spirit and veins of the voters there. In the end it was in the count.

Edwards's people totaled 89, and with only 30 votes the Biden group was too small to be viable. They could either leave the caucus or realign themselves with one of the viable groups. A few of them stormed out of the front doors while others were being persuaded to join the various groups. Thirty minutes was allotted for this process called "wrangling."[16]

[16] James Q. Lynch, "What Happens at a Caucus?" *The Gazette*, November 17, 2007 [http://web.archive.org/web/20071222142101/http://www.iowacaucus.com/apps/pbcs.dll/article?AID=/20071119/IOWACAUCUS/71119004].

People had been there for over an hour now. Many of them had arrived before 6:30, and they were getting tired. I stood up and stretched and to give up my seat for folks to rest their coats. Small conversations emerged as the various precinct captains tried to wrangle voters over to their respective sides.

I stood back, with one eye on the children and the other observing the crowd. The Edwards people were clearly the hardworking, blue-collar, chapped-hands folks. Many of them were factory and mill workers, and judging from their tee-shirts, were also proud union members. The Obama group was quite a contrast. As I talked to some of the people around me, I learned that many of them were young, college-educated professionals. I met an elementary school teacher who was married to an engineer, a human resources manager from Cargill, and two IT administrators. The differences between the statistics reflected in the flesh. These were real people taking part in a real political process, standing before their neighbors, and coworkers, and bosses, and church members, and pastors, and children; raising their hands – whether hardened and calloused or soft and manicured – those raised hands in that room at that moment were equal and carried the same weight. And I stood witness to this whole phenomenon called a caucus.

The time had come for the final count. Most of the Kucinich people left. The Richardson, Dodd and Biden people had either left or joined other groups. The final counted ended up totaling 335: 75 for Hillary; 111 for Edwards; 149 for Obama. He'd won! He'd gained 4 of the 9 delegates. Edwards got 3, and Hillary got 2. We realized that not only had we won, but had kicked Hillary's butt in the process! The mood on the Obama side was exuberant. There were hugs and handshakes and thank-you's from the parents of the children I'd watched. People began breaking into little congratulatory clumps that eventually disbanded and disappeared through the city hall doors. I joined up with Norma, and we waited for Mark to bring around the car. We dropped her off at home and thanked her for caucusing and helping Obama win the precinct. Mark and I immediately let out a big shout and gave each other a high-five, shouting, "We did it! We did it! We did it!"

We didn't have to explain or say what "it" was. "It" was history. "It" was the closest the country had come to electing a black man as president of the United States. We were pumped. We flipped out our cell phones and began calling loved ones. My first call was to Denise.

"Hey girl! I just left a caucus. We kicked Hillary's butt!" I shouted. She laughed.

Mark talked to someone on his cell phone as he drove towards downtown Cedar Rapids, heading for the 16th floor of the Crowne Plaza, to the Obama reception that had quickly become the victory party. The room was big and too warm. I spotted "Team Indy" (a group of college kids from Indianapolis) at one of the table rounds near the front of the room. We greeted each other with smiles and hugs and quick exchanges of what happened at our caucus sites. I listened as I peeled away layers of clothes – James's scarf, my coat, my jacket, my Obama headband. I halfway listened to Team Indy. I wanted a cool drink and to call home. Their stories ended, and I excused myself. I spotted some canned sodas on ice on my way out of the ballroom and grabbed a Sprite. I called my sister, Debra. She answered the phone screaming. Returns were beginning to come across the television, and CNN had projected Obama the winner. My heart was racing as I hung up the phone, and I couldn't stop smiling. I dialed James.

"Hi, sweetie," he said into the telephone.

"Hey! Didya hear the news?"

"No, I just finished up a GED presentation at Truman College," he explained. "What happened?"

"Barack won Iowa! He won!" I shouted into the phone.

He exploded with laughter and congratulations.

I called my mother. She was lying in bed and was a little groggy. I was excited and becoming hoarse.

"Hey, Mommie!"

"Hey, Chelle."

"Turn on the TV," I whispered.

"What's going on?" she responded sleepily.

"Turn on the news, Mommie. Obama won Iowa!"

She did. WGN was announcing Obama's victory. She laughed and told me to enjoy the celebration, that we had earned it. She then told me how very proud she was of me.

I hung up feeling good inside – deep down inside. We'd done it. Nine long days of canvassing and phone-banking; of rejection and maybe-so's; of tired feet and aching backs; of chapped lips and nearly frost-bitten fingers; of hopes wavering up and down – and through it all, we'd done it. The volunteers from out of state working with the local teams on the ground in Iowa, we'd gotten out the vote, and the people of Iowa had spoken. They wanted change. They voted for Barack Obama on the Democratic side and Mike Huckabee on the Republican.

I rejoined the party in the ballroom. Marla and Ann Marie and their children were there. So were Zett and Beth, Carol and Elden, Jeff, and Anthony, and Lauren, and Doug. I saw April Harley from the Finance Team at the Chicago headquarters, and Shira and her dad, Mark – the guy who'd driven me and Norma to the caucus. I saw so many people, many of whom I didn't know and others whom I'd met during the trip. The room was hot. The mood was euphoric. We were all on a super high.

The waitstaff began setting out pizzas. The bars were buzzing with people ordering beers. Suddenly, a hush fell over the room. The lights lowered, and the projector screen came to life. And there he was – Barack Obama, larger than life, his image filling the room. He was speaking from Des Moines, Iowa. He was thanking all of the voters and volunteers and staff and supporters. He spoke about his vision of hope for America – *"where ordinary people can do extraordinary things, when they work together towards that common goal."* He spoke about how Americans can reclaim our government and become engaged in it again; how each of us – no matter what color, what ideology, what religion, whether a red state or blue state, together we could help rebuild these United States. He reminded us that the victory on *"this night, at this moment, was the beginning of making history – and that each of us was a part of and witness to it."* His speech was the best yet.

The ballroom erupted into applause and hugs, tears and shouts and sounds so alive and passionate until they seemed to form shapes. People began taking pictures of the large screen. We took pictures of each other. I hugged people I didn't know, and they hugged me back. Obama's speech had moved us all. He spoke from his heart to ours, and we felt it. At that moment we were all brothers and sisters, one big happy family. We held on to those feelings for a while and captured them through photographs. We resumed eating and drinking, laughing and flirting. Many names and numbers were exchanged that night. New friendships and contacts were created. I, Lauren, Anthony and Team Indy took a picture together – freezing that moment in time forever.

The party began breaking up around midnight. I wasn't sure of how I was getting back to the hotel, or whom I'd be riding back to Chicago with in the morning. I didn't care, either. God had watched over me thus far, and I knew he was watching over me, over us, especially over Barack, that night. I sat back and smiled, finished my beer and waited on the right time, opportunity, and person to take me home. Two college kids I'd seen at the Super 8 passed by my table and said "No problem" when I asked for a lift. I smiled. God was definitely watching over me, over Iowa, over the Obama family, over the American family.

❧

THE TRIP HOME

The euphoria I'd felt on my first day in Iowa had returned for my last. I still wasn't sure of how I was getting home. I only knew that Mike Jordan, an Obama worker who was also staying at the Super 8, had assured me that he'd find a ride. That was enough for me. I felt too good to be worried about anything. At about 9:30 that morning, Mike had secured a ride for me with a couple who lived in New Lenox – a southwest suburb of Chicago. They were pulling out at 10 a.m.

I rode back with Pam and Addison and Dave. We talked about our canvassing and caucus experiences, and took turns reading snippets and statistics from various newspapers to each other.

"Upset in Iowa!" one headline blared. "Obama Wins!" read another.

"By what percentage did the *Times* say Obama beat Clinton?" Pam inquired.

"By eight percent," Dave cheerily responded. "In other words, he whooped her ass!"

We laughed and drank coffee, shared more stories and smiled. After a couple of hours, a hush replaced our chatter. We each sat silently, reflecting on the previous week's events. The sun penetrated the car windows and warmed us through and through. I gazed out at the snow-covered Illinois landscape and smiled. As close as I was to home, I was a million miles away and indulged myself in wishful thinking. My mind was light-years ahead into the future: where a black man was the leader of the free world; into a further future where my great-nieces and great-great-nephews would live wherever they wished, learn all that their hearts desired, travel as citizens of the world, and love and marry whomever they fell in love with. I envisioned a world of relative peace, where respect replaced resentment and brotherhood trumped statehood. We'd taken a small step in that direction with the win in Iowa, and still we had a very long way to go. I gazed out of the window, looking beyond the dormant cornfields and occasional farmhouses, past the cars sailing by in the opposite direction, and into the future. I smiled at the possibilities, and knew at that moment that transforming the impossible began with hope. I was filled with it. Hope had gotten me to and through Iowa, and hope was carrying me home now. I prayed that Barack would win more primaries and go on to win the Democratic nomination. I prayed that he'd be our next president. At that moment, I prayed and held on to hope.

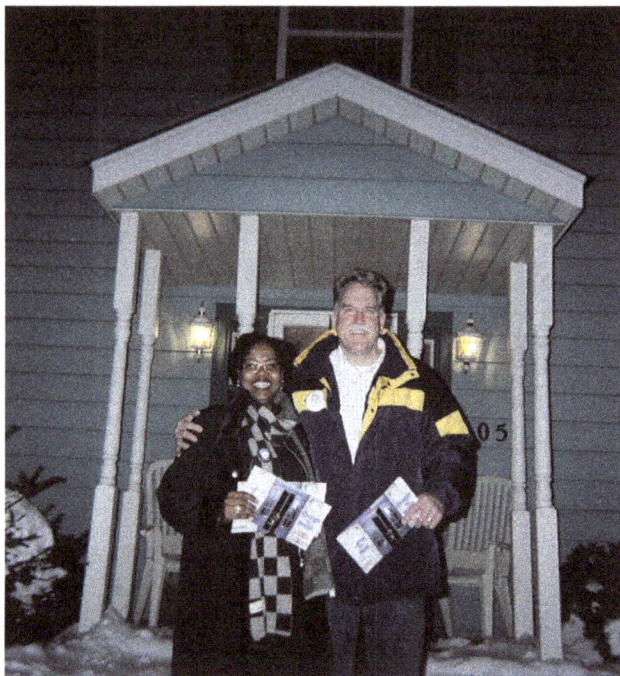

Bob and me after a long night of canvassing in
Cedar Rapids, Iowa.

Outside Dave and Lisa's "station house" ready to canvass with Doug, intern
from Texas (the guy without a coat).

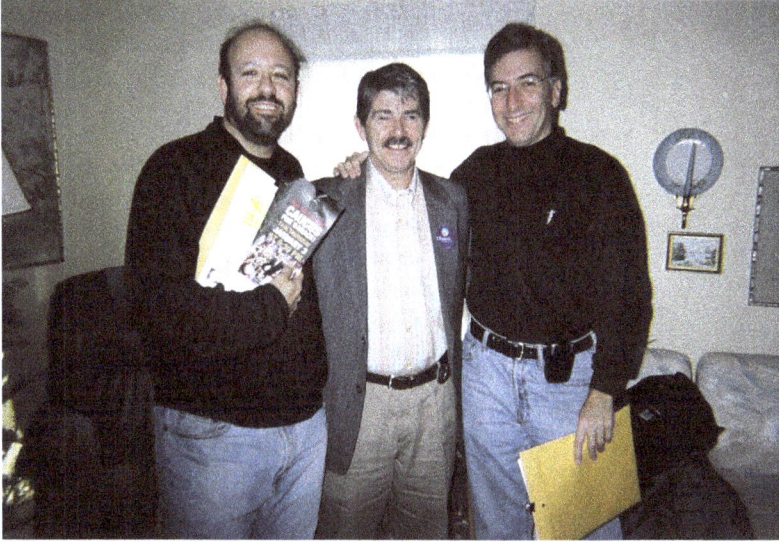

Former Chicago Mayor David Orr sharing a light moment with other volunteers before hitting the streets of Cedar Rapids.

The Iowa GOTV volunteers, including "Team Indy" celebrate Obama's victory in Iowa.

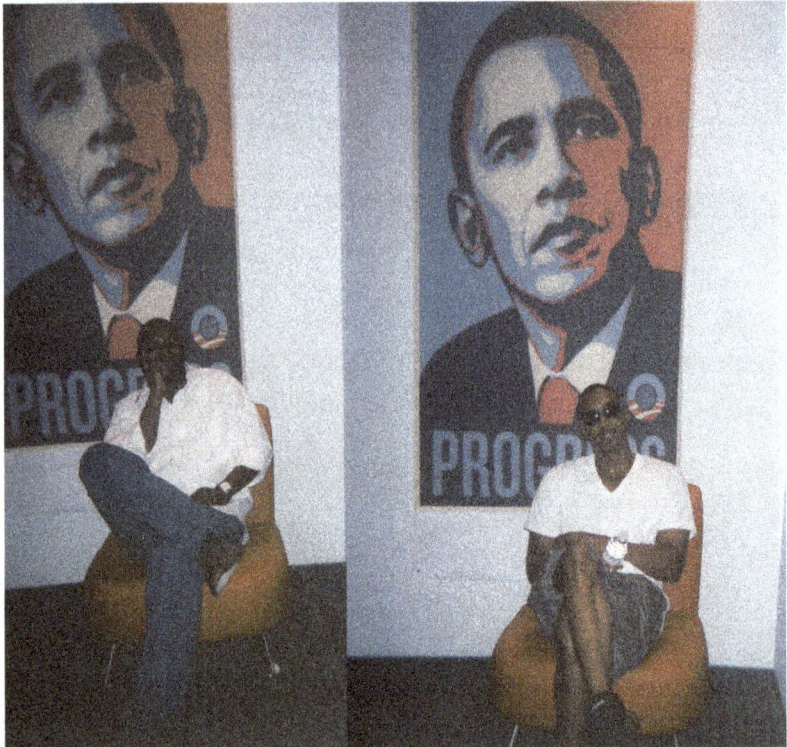

My nephews, Alfonso Daniel and Edward Clay, representing my "Atlanta Grassroots Fundraising Delegation," getting a private tour of the National Headquarters in Chicago on July 4, 2008.

Me, teen volunteers and our mothers in the Flossmoor, Illinois parade,
September 2008.

CHAPTER
Four
RACE, THE REVEREND, AND THE ROAD
TO DENVER

REVEREND WRIGHT

Obama's win in Iowa catapulted him to the front of the pack of Democratic presidential hopefuls. Clinton retaliated with an upset win in New Hampshire and took back the lead. The race on the Democratic side was tight and fierce. Depending on the week, either Obama, Clinton or Edwards led. By mid-March each of the campaigns was beginning to tire and make its share of mistakes and snafus. When Geraldine Ferraro, a former vice presidential nominee of the 1984 presidential election campaign and current member of Clinton's finance committee, stated on national television, "If Obama was a white man, he would not be in this position. And if he was a woman (of any color) he would not be in this position. He happens to be very lucky to be who he is. And the country is caught up in the concept."

Clinton was knocked from her lead position, and Obama resumed the top spot. That was on Wednesday, March 12th. The next day began the long weekend of Reverend Jeremiah Wright, Jr. – Obama's former pastor – and the ascent of Clinton back to the top.

It was a Thursday evening and I did my usual – catch the 8:20 p.m. commuter train home after working at the college in the morning and campaign headquarters in the evening. Nothing out of the ordinary.

The train swooshed through tunnels and past skyscrapers, blocking the signal on my ringing cell phone. I got home, changed into comfortable bum-around-the-house-clothes, grabbed a soda and settled into my favorite chair. Normal Thursday stuff. I clicked on the television remote. The picture on the old Philips TV slowly filled in. And there it was, a fuzzy video portrayal of an angry Rev. Wright shouting.

"No, not GOD BLESS America! But, GOD D**N AMERICA!"

"What!" I coughed up through a swig of 7-Up. "What?"

". . . and in this country of the U.S. of KKK-A!" a blurb from another sermon announced.

"Oh my God," I gulped, my heart sinking.

"NO, NO, NO! GOD D**N AMERICA! That's in the Bible for killing innocent people. GOD D**N AMERICA for treating our citizens as less than human. GOD D**N AMERICA for as long as she acts like she is God and she is supreme!"[17]

The old lion strode through the pulpit, pointing and shouting. The caption beneath the video clip read: *Jeremiah Wright, Jr., Democratic Presidential Candidate Barack Obama's Pastor.*

"Oh God," I sighed.

I retreated to the couch, where I practically stayed all weekend. Flat on my back with the television muted, but unable to turn it off or away from the endless video montage of sermon snippets playing ad nauseam on the cable channels, and network news channels, and newspaper headlines, the entire weekend. They made me tired. They made me sad. They made me mad. *This isn't happening*, I told myself. This was not the Rev. Wright I'd heard so much about over the years. I was born and raised on the South Side of Chicago and could recall the whole hullabaloo about the new progressive church being built on 95th Street – Trinity United Church of Christ. I remembered when my college friends Audrey and Morris got married there in the early eighties; when Kevin, a friend and former coworker, joined the church and started dating a

---

[17] Brian Ross and Rehab El-Bari, "Obama's Pastor: God Damn America, U. S. to Blame for 9/11," ABC News, March 13, 2008. [http://abcnews.go.com/Blotter/DemocraticDebate/story?id=4443788&page=1]

woman whom he almost married. I remember hearing about this church that fed poor people and clothed homeless men and families; about this powerful preacher who was resurrecting the emotionally dead and down-trodden with his passionate preaching of self-awareness. Something was not right here. These snippets weren't representative of the Barack Obama I'd come to know and admire and had worked hard for, nor of the people I'd met at campaign headquarters who were also members of Trinity. But the video clips wouldn't stop, especially on Fox News. Over and over, all weekend. And when they did hit the pause button on the videos themselves, the newscasters denigrated Obama and called for him to pull out of the race.

I lay on the couch, ignoring my ringing phone, grumbling stomach, and thirst for water. I couldn't seem to move. I thought about all of the time, energy, money and effort I'd poured into this campaign, into some-thing and someone that I really believed in. I thought about all of the people I'd encouraged to get involved in the American electoral process. *And for what? This?*

What I was seeing and hearing on television just didn't square with the personal knowledge and relationships I had with the people of that church. My head was swimming with questions: Why did Rev. Wright have to say those things in that way? Didn't he know the sermons were taped? Didn't he understand that others wouldn't understand? Couldn't he foresee what would happen? No. I answered myself. Who could have foreseen this? While one side of me understood his anger and frustra-tion with fighting against injustice and racism and poverty, the other side kept asking "why" because I understood that people outside of these situations wouldn't understand what in the hell he was shouting about. Why was this happening? Why was Rev. Wright being portrayed this way? Why, over the course of his long tenure as a pastor, were only these snippets of his most fiery sermons being paraded repeatedly? Why was Obama being silent? Where was Obama?

"Oh, Lord. Help us." I prayed.

A text message alert beeped on my phone. It was James. His message simply read: "Now is not the time to quit. Hang in there. Stay strong."

I hadn't talked to him since this whole story broke. How did he know how deflated I was? I guessed because he felt much the same. I stared at the words and cried. Tears streamed down my face as I felt equal amounts of guilt and embarrassment. I'd pretty much surmised that white folks would in no way understand what was happening in that church or in that community. And through the wonder of phone technology, I was drinking in the soothing words of a very special white guy who not only knew how I felt, but knew what to say to my heart. I cried so hard until I laughed. I laughed to ease the pain. I clutched the phone to my chest and cried myself to sleep.

Monday morning came. The alarm clock went off at 6 a.m. I banged it off and lay there with puffy eyes and a heavy heart. For the first time, I regretted having to go to the campaign headquarters. I thought about calling in sick, which wouldn't have been an untruth. I was sick to my stomach with fear of the angry voices I'd have to encounter on the telephones. I didn't want to face the music of angry supporters. I didn't want to hear the vitriol from non-supporters. I pulled the bedcovers over my ears. I thought about quitting, just calling up Liz and letting her know that I couldn't do this anymore. How was I to explain how Obama could simultaneously be close to Rev. Wright spiritually, yet distant from him philosophically? How does one explain away the complicated issue of race in America via a bumper-sticker sound bite or carefully crafted phone scripts? How could I answer the myriad of justifiably angry questions that awaited me? The best thing to do was to quit the campaign. Pick up the phone and call Liz. I reached for my cell phone and stopped. "Now is not the time to quit," I heard James's voice say. I snatched my hand back. *Damn him*, I thought. *As usual, he's right.*

THE CALLS

"WHAT THE HELL KINDA PREACHER IS THIS REV. WRIGHT DUDE," an angry white voice shouted from the other end of the phone. "WHAT KINDA SCAM ARE YOU FOLKS RUNNING UP THERE?"

The tongue lashing had begun.

"Obama for America. This is Michelle. How may I . . ." is all I managed before the caller cut in.

"HOW COULD OBAMA SIT THERE YEAR AFTER YEAR FOR TWENTY YEARS AND LISTEN TO THAT VILE," the caller screamed. "HOW CAN YOU STILL BE SUPPORTING SOMEBODY LIKE THAT? HUH, HOW COULD YOU?"

I couldn't answer the caller. I had no sound bite answer, and surprisingly the campaign didn't have scripts for us either. They'd advised us to listen to the callers, let them speak and express themselves. They'd advised us to be apologetic for upsetting supporters, but not to apologize for the Obama family belonging to the church. *Yeah, but how do I do that?* I wondered as I answered each angry call.

"HOW IN THE HELL CAN OBAMA BELONG TO THAT CHURCH! TALKING 'BOUT HOPE AND PEACE OUTTA ONE SIDE OF HIS MOUTH AND AGREEING WITH THAT PREACHER OUTTA THE OTHER? I WANT MY MONEY BACK FROM THAT SHYSTER!"

"Sir, I'm sorry. . ."

"YEAH, YEAH YOU'RE SORRY. I. WANT. MY. MONEY. BACK!"

"Yes, sir. I can transfer you over to our Finance Department."

"YEAH, YOU DO THAT! AND I'M TELLING ALL OF MY FRIENDS TO GET THEIR MONEY BACK TOO! F*_*K OBAMA!"

I transferred the call and hung my head. The Call Center was sharing space with the Correspondence Department, which handled all of the written correspondence. A few of the staff looked away as they overheard my end of the interrupted conversation. A couple others gave me sympathetic looks. One guy told me to "hang in there."

"HOW LONG OBAMA BEEN SITTING IN THAT CHURCH LISTENING TO THAT S*_*T? HUH, HOW LONG? YEARS! THAT'S HOW LONG. HE IS A RACIST PIG! AND, I'M NEVER GOING TO VOTE FOR HIS SKINNY LITTLE BLACK A** NOW! Y'ALL CAN FORGET IT! THIS CAMPAIGN IS OVER, BABY!"

"Well, sir. . ."

"I AIN'T SPENDING ANOTHER DIME ON NO NIGGAS LIKE THIS! WHERE THE F*_*K IS MY MONEY! GIVE ME MY GOD*_*N MONEY BACK!"

"Yes, sir."

And that's how it went, call after call, on and on. And when I wasn't talking to angry callers, I took on the queries of disheartened ones.

"I'm calling from Portland, Oregon," the caller started nervously. "I'm a white gay man, and I really stuck my neck out for Obama." There was a long pause, and then a crack in the caller's voice indicated that he was crying. "I really stuck my neck out here, getting people involved in this campaign. Well, all is lost now. I feel so betrayed. What do I say? What do I do? I-I'm sorry I ever got involved in all of this. I-I-I'm sorry."

The caller hung up before I could tell him that I was sorry too, before I could try to make him understand all of this. I rubbed my throbbing forehead. My whole head was swimming with pain and grief. I looked around at the solemn faces of the other volunteers. We were getting our butts kicked with calls. There were only five of us answering phones that morning. Normally, there would have been double that amount. Three people had called off. Two hadn't even bothered. I hated to bail out, but I needed some fresh air. Liz was hanging right in there with us. When she wasn't on the phone with a caller, she was answering complaints coming in via email. She looked in my direction and gave me the signal to mute my phone and take a break. I'd been on the phones for nearly two hours and was pretty well beaten up. I grabbed my purse and coat and headed outside for a long smoke and to try to think clearly.

That last caller had really upset me. He sounded desperately weary. The range of emotions had gone from punch-you-in-face anger to disappointment to sadness to hints of suicide. The campaign had gone from hope-filled to hopelessness. I stood outside leaning against a steel beam, closed my eyes, letting the Chicago winter air chill my face and clear my head. *Obama's gotta fix this*, I thought. *What do we tell people? He's gotta do something, or all of those callers are right. This campaign is over.*

I returned to the office and saw that two more volunteers had come in. Liz was off the phones. In fact, most of the people were off the phones. They'd been ringing like crazy earlier. Now they weren't.

"What's up, Liz?" I asked.

"The news stations are reporting that Obama is going to speak on this whole Reverend Wright issue."

"Thank God!"

"Yeah, it's been pretty rough. Thanks for being such a trooper, Michelle."

"No problem," I lied. "When is Obama speaking?"

"Uh, tomorrow, I think," Liz said absentmindedly between eyeing her email and texting somebody else.

That was my cue to get back to the phones, if they started ringing again. All of America must have been watching the breaking news announcements and decided to give the phones a break. It was both magical and eerie. And suddenly, they started ringing again.

"The news is saying that Obama gonna speak tomorrow. Is that true?"

"I believe so, ma'am," I answered the caller. "We're just getting the information, too."

"Well, I sure hope so. It's a big ole mess down here in South Carolina," the elderly woman said with a sigh.

"I know. It's a big ole mess up here, too," I replied.

The breaking news really helped. The occasional angry call still came through, but the tenor of the calls had definitely changed.

"Hang in there, baby. It ain't over 'til it's over," a young man with a New York accent said. "Tell Obama to hang tough. We still got his back out here in New York."

"Thank you, sir," I replied.

"Let me tell you something, baby," another elderly black woman with a southern accent was saying. "I'm eighty-six years old and done seen lots of things in my time. I know what that reverend is talking 'bout. I just wish things was different, but they ain't. Ain't nothing we can do 'bout that. I just wanted to call to tell y'all not to give up. Obama is a blessed child. I knows it. 'Sho as I know the back my hands. Tell him not to give up. Tell him to pray. Tell him to give a good speech tomorrow. Will you tell him that for me, sugar?"

"Yes, ma'am, I will."

"Thank ya, baby. Y'all keep ya heads up high. We's praying for you down here in Mississippi."

"Thank you, ma'am. We appreciate your prayers. What part of Mississippi?" I asked.

"Greenwood. You know it?"

"Yes, ma'am. My family is from Greenville."

"Well, bless your heart! You stay sweet, sugar, and tell Obama we's praying for him."

"Yes, ma'am. It'll be my pleasure."

And it was. The caller had made my day. She reminded me of my grandmother, Arveal Robinson. It made me temporarily forget how bad the morning had been. I took real pleasure in typing out the phone message and forwarding it to Liz, who forwarded condensed messages to Correspondence, who in turn sent summaries of good and bad messages to Obama's chief of staff. I hoped Obama would get her message and prayer. I hoped her prayers and the many others would help the campaign. Perhaps all wasn't lost. Perhaps the campaign wasn't over. And just perhaps, in the days to come, Obama would be on the top perch again.

THE RACE SPEECH

I'll never forget March 18, 2008. Not only was it Mom's 72nd birthday, and her spirits and health were in high gear, but it was also the date that Obama gave what became known as his "best speech" ever – dubbed *The Race Speech*. My Aunt Ellen and my brother, Calvin Clay from Dallas, were at the house celebrating Mom's birthday. We'd eaten and opened gifts and, like the rest of the world, awaited Obama's speech that evening.

Aunt Ellen and I sat on the living floor leaning against the sofa, hugging our knees. Calvin, whom I suspected was not an Obama supporter, sat on the love seat opposite us with pretty much a "so what" expression on his face. The press conference was beginning and Obama approached the lectern. Aunt Ellen folded her hands as if in prayer. Mom smiled. Calvin asked a question. I was nervous. I hoped that Obama would be able to stop the hemorrhage of abandoning campaign supporters with his words tonight. Silence fell over the house as he began to speak. We listened intently.

"We the people, in order to form a more perfect union. Two hundred and twenty one years ago, in a hall that still stands across the street, a group of men gathered and, with these simple words, launched America's improbable experiment in democracy."

Aunt Ellen and I leaned forward, drinking in his every word. We turned towards one another and smiled a smile that said "Good start. Keep going, brother." He did.

"The document they produced was eventually signed but ultimately unfinished. It was stained by this nation's original sin of slavery. . ."

"Amen, brother," Aunt Ellen whispered.

"Go ahead, Barack!" I shouted.

Mom shushed us. Calvin wrinkled his brow.

"Of course, the answer to the slavery question was already embedded within our Constitution – a Constitution that had at is very core the ideal of equal citizenship under the law; a Constitution that promised its people liberty, and justice, and a union that could be and should be perfected over time.

"And yet words on a parchment would not be enough to deliver slaves from bondage, or provide men and women of every color and creed their full rights and obligations as citizens of the United States."

"That's right!" Aunt Ellen said.

"This was one of the tasks we set forth at the beginning of this presidential campaign – to continue the long march of those who came before us, a march for a more just, more equal, more free, more caring and more prosperous America. I chose to run for president at this moment in history because I believe deeply that we cannot solve the challenges of our time unless we solve them together. . . . This belief comes from my unyielding faith in the decency and generosity of the American people. But it also comes from my own story."

"Bless you, brother," I said towards the television.

"Amen, amen," Aunt Ellen cosigned.

"Shushhh!" Mom insisted.

"I am the son of a black man from Kenya and a white woman from Kansas. I was raised with the help of a white grandfather who survived a Depression to serve in Patton's Army during World War II and a white grandmother who worked on a bomber assembly line at Fort Leavenworth while he was overseas. I've gone to some of the best schools in America and lived in one of the world's poorest nations. I am married to a black American who carries within her the blood of slaves and slave owners – an inheritance we pass on to our two precious daughters. I have brothers, sisters, nieces, nephews, uncles and cousins of every race and every hue, scattered across three continents, and for as long as I live, I will never forget that in no other country on Earth is my story even possible."

We couldn't hold back, not even Mom. We screamed and high-fived and hugged and were on the verge of tears listening to the words, watching him paint the picture of American race relations. And Obama was the perfect person to deliver the words that were being said.

"That brother is bad!" Aunt Ellen said, slapping her thigh.

"Bad to da bone, baby!" I agreed as we high-fived.

"Three continents! Lord have mercy," Mom added.

Calvin sat at attention, but silent. With a slight roll of the eyes, his look – one that I'd seen many times over the years – simply said, "women?"

Mom brought us all back to order, "Shush, y'all. Let's listen."

"Throughout the first year of this campaign, against all predictions to the contrary, we saw how hungry the American people were for this message of unity. . . This is not to say that race has not been an issue in this campaign. . . we've heard my former pastor, Jeremiah Wright, use incendiary language to express views that have the potential not only to widen the racial divide, but views that denigrate both the greatness and the goodness of our nation, and that rightly offend white and black alike.

"I have already condemned, in unequivocal terms, the statements of Reverend Wright that have caused such controversy and, in some cases, pain.

"Reverend Wright's comments were not only wrong but divisive, divisive at a time when we need unity; racially charged at a time when we need to come together to solve a set of monumental problems – two wars, a terrorist threat, a falling economy, a chronic health care crisis and potentially devastating climate change – problems that are neither black nor white nor Latino nor Asian, but rather problems that confront us all.

"*Given my background, my politics, and my professed values and ideals, there will no doubt be those for whom my statements of condemnation are not enough. Why associate myself with Reverend Wright in the first place, they may ask? Why not join another church? And I confess that if all that I knew of Reverend Wright were the snippets of those sermons that have run in an endless loop on the television sets and YouTube, or if Trinity United Church of Christ conformed to the caricatures being peddled by some commentators, there is no doubt that I would react in much the same way.*

"*But the truth is, that isn't all that I know of the man. The man I met more than twenty years ago is a man who helped introduce me to my Christian faith, a man who spoke to me about our obligations to love one another, to care for the sick and lift up the poor. He is a man who served his country as a United States Marine; who has studied and lectured at some of the finest universities and seminaries in the country, and who for over thirty years has led a church that serves the community by doing God's work here on Earth – by housing the homeless, ministering to the needy, providing day care services and scholarships and prison ministries, and reaching out to those suffering from HIV/AIDS.*

"*And this helps explain, perhaps, my relationship with Reverend Wright. As imperfect as he may be, he has been like family to me. He strengthened my faith, officiated my wedding, and baptized my children. Not once in my conversations with him have I heard him talk about any ethnic group in derogatory terms, or treat whites with whom he interacted with anything but courtesy and respect. He contains within him the contradictions – the good and the bad – of the community that he has served diligently for so many years.*

"*I can no more disown him than I can disown the black community. I can no more disown him than I can disown my white grandmother – a woman who helped raise me, a woman who sacrificed again and again for me, a woman who loves me as much as she loves anything in this world, but a woman who once confessed her fear of black men who passed her by on the street, and who on more than one occasion has uttered racial or ethnic stereotypes that made me cringe.*

"*These people are a part of me. And they are part of America, this country that I love.*"[18]

---

[18] Excerpts from the transcript, "Barack Obama's Speech On Race," *New York Times*, March 18, 2008 [http://abcnews.go.com/Blotter/DemocraticDebate/story?id=4443788&page=1

The tears began rolling down my face. I watched Obama, a scrawny but strong man, lift the weight of America's ugly race relations onto his back and shoulder the issue with Herculean strength. He spoke with passion and honesty, quiet at times, fiery at others. There was nothing stiff, phony, staged or professorial in how he delivered the words. He spoke from the heart. He spoke to my heart. I looked around our living room. He spoke to my family's heart – including my brother Calvin. Aunt Ellen had become teary-eyed. Mom was slowly rubbing my back in that soothing way that she does to say, "Go on child. Let it out. It's gonna all be all right."

And she was correct. It was going to be all right. Not only had Obama stopped the hemorrhaging, but he'd applied salve to the wound. I'm sure just like mine, nearly every household in the country was talking, or crying, or hugging, or reacting in some way to the speech he'd just given. I looked at my family and smiled through my tears. Mom continued to rub my back. I turned slightly towards her and whispered, "Happy birthday, Mom."

᧯

August 23, 2008

Dear Journal,

I can hardly believe that just two weeks ago I finished a video shoot for the Obama campaign. Chris Hughes himself sent me an email asking if I'd be interested in being the "voice" of an everyday person on the Grassroots Finance Committee. "Interested" was an understatement. I was honored. The shoot went well, and the video was subsequently blasted out across the country to the massive OFA supporter email list, embedded in a fundraising message from Campaign Manager David Plouffe.[19] I've become a small-time celebrity around the headquarters and with my family and friends, for the moment anyway. And now this – Denver-bound, heading to the Democratic National Convention!

I'm up early because I couldn't sleep. I leave for Denver this afternoon, part of the Credentials Team for the "Obama Friends and Family." I don't quite know what that means or the totality of the work involved, but I'm going. I'm on this incredible journey for the long haul, no matter what. My bags are packed and sitting near the front door. I've had my coffee and a light breakfast, and now I'm waiting – on time. I've gone through my mental checklist of whether I've packed all of the necessities for the trip:

o *Toiletries, face and body care products – check;*

o *Disposable cameras – check;*

o *Coordinated jewelry – check;*

o *Walking shoes – check;*

o *Tuxedo shirt from James to wear to Invesco Field – big check!*

෴

---

[19] The link to the GFC campaign video clip is: http://www.youtube.com/watch?v=kmvJvHRo3VM, or by searching YouTube by typing in "Michelle Carnes" and "GFC."

CHAPTER

Five

DENVER

THE DEMOCRATIC NATIONAL CONVENTION

"Welcome to Frontier Airways flight number 533 to Denver, Colorado! General boarding will begin shortly!" I boarded the plane and reclined my seat slightly after takeoff. I closed my eyes and reminisced about the first presidential election in which I'd participated. It was 1976, thirty-two years ago: Carter vs. Ford. I was a neophyte Young Democrat then, eyes lit with the excitement of being a living part of what I'd read about in social studies and civics classes. Back then, I'd stuffed and licked envelopes, taped campaign literature to doorknobs and mailboxes, and run other errands as needed or directed by older, senior Democrats. Now I chuckled inside at how times had changed. This time, the primary mode of communication was via the Internet – emails, fundraising, event planning and voter registration. Back then, working a campaign was more face-to-face and physical, but now licking envelopes was out. This time, the election was being fueled from the ground up, not organized and mandated from the top down. Just like before, I was still walking the campaign trail, canvassing neighborhoods, making phone calls and attending fundraisers, but this time my party leaders and bosses were people young enough to be my children. *How refreshing*, I thought. *How encouraging.* Those thoughts made me feel young again, like the wide-eyed, idealistic teenager I'd been all those many years ago. I held on to those thoughts, letting the sun warm my face, drifting in and out of nostalgia until I dozed off, with my last thought being that Jimmy Carter won that year.

I awoke to the crackly announcement by the pilot: "Ladies and gentlemen, we're beginning our descent into Denver." I pulled my seat forward and peered out the window, looking at the grassy and mountainous landscape below. As the plane began touching down, the past was also reaching out towards the present. Thirty-two years is a long time, but here I was again on the ground, at the center of another presidential election, hoping, praying, and working hard to push fate towards putting victory in the Democratic column.

THE DEMOCRATIC NATIONAL CONVENTION: AN OVERVIEW

The Westin Hotel in downtown Denver was the host hotel and headquarters for the 2008 Democratic National Convention, so all Obama staff, the Obama family and extended family, and other officials and dignitaries stayed there. This was also my assigned work location for the next five days.

It was a beautiful hotel, an emerald granite building featuring large, greenish windows and brushed steel. The credentials office, on the mezzanine level, was set up on the order of an old-fashioned bank teller's counter without the bars. Long black drapes on tubular frames divided the mezzanine into several sections: a lounge area with small tables and chairs; food and beverage stations; a long row of meeting rooms; and small, temporary offices set up for Obama staff. On our first day, staffers from the Democratic National Committee (DNC) were on hand to explain how the convention would work, and to give a general overview of the purpose of having a convention in the first place. The information they provided answered many of the myriad questions that friends, family and voters along the campaign trail had, or would, ask me:

1. What is the DNC?

Although the acronym DNC would seem to stand for Democratic National Convention, it actually is the abbreviation for the Democratic National Committee, which is the Democratic Party's national organization.

2. What does the DNC do?

Among other responsibilities such as providing national leadership for the party, coordinating fundraising and election strategies (like the "50-State" strategy executed by Chairman Howard Dean for the 2008 election), and promoting the party's platform of ideas and planned actions, the DNC's convention responsibilities include:

- °   Choosing a permanent chairperson for the convention;
- °   Choosing the convention site;
- °   Designating a person to kick off the convention and provide the keynote address;
- °   Deciding how many delegates each state may send to the convention.[20]

3. What happens at a convention?

The main goals of the convention are to:

- °   Nominate the presidential and vice residential candidates;
- °   Establish the party platform; and
- °   Unify the party after oftentimes hard-fought primary battles

Other official business of the convention includes:

- °   Accepting the credentials of the state delegates;
- °   Seating the delegates;
- °   Ratifying the rules of the various convention committees; and
- °   Electing the officers.[21]

4. Who are delegates and superdelegates?

- °   Delegates are the people at the national convention who do the actual voting to nominate the presidential and vice presidential

---

[20] Different sources were consulted to compile a listing of similar functions performed by national conventions. For a detailed accounting of convention activities see William Crotty and John S. Jackson III, *Presidential Primaries and Nominations* (Washington, D. C.: CQ Press, 1985), ch. 8. For an overview of the general functions of a party convention see "Political Convention," *World Book* (Chicago: World Book, Inc.) 2006, V 15, pp. 628-630.

[21] Ibid.

candidates. Delegates can be either pledged or unpledged (commonly called "superdelegates"). The difference between the two is as follows:

○ Pledge delegates must vote for specific presidential candidates at the national convention and are usually bound by the results of the state's presidential primary or caucus. About 80 percent of the Democratic delegates are pledged.

○ Unpledged delegates are by definition "free agents" who are not bound by the results of state primaries or caucuses. They can vote for whomever they like at the national convention, and are generally high-profile elected officials or distinguished party leaders, such as former presidents or vice presidents, former U.S. Senate leaders, or U. S. House Speakers.[22]

I, along with Joyce, June, Judy and Yvonne, made up the Chicago delegation of volunteers from the National Headquarters that had been hand-selected by Bridget Gray, the OFA Credentials Coordinator. Our assignment was to work with her on the prized "Obama Friends and Family" Credentials Team. Those of us in the room all pretty much understood the big picture of conventions. The piece in the puzzle that I really needed to get a firm grasp on was how the various credentials departments figured into the whole process. After a couple of days of watching, working and listening, I came to understand just how germane credentials were to the smooth operation of the convention itself. They were the lifeblood of access to convention events. No credential, no entry, no exceptions. Those glossy little pieces of cardstock paper with colorful images and embossed date stamps gained the bearer entry into closed meetings, ticketed public speeches, access in and out of hotels; and like a backstage pass to a rock-n-roll concert, certain credentials garnered entry to exclusive and elusive private parties. And of all of the credentials-issuing units, the "Obama Friends and Family" credentials department was the place to be.

[22] Delegate Types Explained," *Boston Globe*, 2008 [http://www.boston.com/news/ politics/2008/primaries/about_national_delegates/].

CREDENTIALS OPERATIONS

There were millions of credentials to be issued to tens of thousands of people attending and participating in the four-day national convention. The major downtown Denver hotels hosted various credentials departments of the DNC or OFA offices. Each hotel had a different credentials responsibility. The setup of daily credentials operations went as follows:

- The Hyatt Hotel issued credentials to the DNC Finance Department, the OFA Finance Department, the OFA Policy and Labor Departments, and to the press. The DNC issued credentials to the delegates at the Sheraton Hotel. The Westin, being the convention's host hotel, handled the credentials of most of the major players and speakers of the convention.

- The "Obama Friends and Family" credentials department dealt with four main groups:

  ° Obama Friends and Family. These were people who were literally friends and family members of Barack and Michelle Obama and Joe and Jill Biden. Family members that I encountered included: Barack's sister, Maya Soetoro-Ng, her husband Konrad and their children; Michelle's mother, Marian Robinson; her brother Craig Robinson, his wife Kelly and his older children, Avery and Leslie; and her godmother, Kaye Wilson. Old college friends of the Obamas, their best friends like Valerie Jarrett and her family, and top surrogates of the campaign, such as Susan Rice and Eric Holder were also part of this group.

  ° Entertainment Celebrities. This group consisted of actors, musicians and other high-profile entertainment and television personalities who were supporting the campaign. Some in this group that I encountered included Hill Harper, Alfre Woodard, Kerry Washington, Jasmine Guy, Holly Robinson-Peete, Blair Underwood, and KeKe Palmer, the young actress from the movie Akeelah and the Bee.

○ The Illinois Delegation. Ken Bennett, the Illinois state director for the campaign, came to the credentials department each morning to sort and label his credentials, and leave them for us to distribute to the respective delegates. Of this group, I encountered Richard M. Daley, mayor of Chicago; Cook County Board of Commissioners President Todd Stroger and his wife Jeanine; Alderman Edward Burke; and former U.S. Representative and person selected to serve as White House Chief of Staff, Rahm Emanuel, and his son.

○ Campaign Staff. This was the last group to which we distributed credentials, and included the top brass of the campaign. People from the national campaign headquarters that I distributed credentials to included: Chief Campaign Strategist David Axelrod, and his wife, Susan; Campaign Manager, David Plouffe, and his family; Steve Hildebrand, Deputy Campaign Manager; Jordan Kaplan, Director of Illinois Finance; April Harley of the Finance Department; and Chris Hughes and Nikki Taylor of MyBo and Grassroots Fundraising.

Transporting the credentials under lock and key to the various hotels was a big job in itself, with the entire process of transporting, receiving, securing and distributing them being quite elaborate. That process went as follows:

- **Delivering the Credentials:** Contracted security companies were retained to keep credentials secured for daily delivery to the various credentials offices. They were accountable items, and valuable including on the black market with values upwards of $1,200 for the August 25th Invesco Field event. So, they were handled very carefully, being transported in large lockboxes that resembled small file cabinets.

- **Receiving and Verifying:** Credentials were delivered each day in the wee hours. Shortly after midnight, Bridget and her small paid staff (both named Melissa) arrived at the office, received and signed for the lockbox, and began counting and verifying the contents. They'd work until two or three in the morning and secured the credentials in the office until their return at 6 a.m.

- **Distributing the Credentials:** We, the volunteers, reported to the credentials office at 7:00 a.m., by which time Bridget and the two Melissas would have obtained "credentials requests" sheets from several departments or units: "Friends and Family" requests; OFA staff requests; Hollywood VIP requests; and from the Illinois delegation. The volunteers would recount and verify Bridget's total; tally up the day's credentials; and open the window, ready to meet and greet the morning gaggle of friends and family who'd convened on the other side of the counter.

Credentials for a day's events could be issued only on that particular date. Because most people got more than just one credential for the day, our office processed and distributed thousands of credentials daily. A couple of days the count was a few thousand; other days it was over eight thousand; and on the day of Barack Obama's speech at Invesco Field, the count swelled to over twelve thousand credentials. Some people, especially the children, only needed one credential, usually to hear the evening speakers at the Pepsi Center. Others, like Mayor Daley or the Emanuel family, needed up to a dozen credentials, depending on how many meetings, different hotels, and evening events and parties they were attending. Because the same bloc of people had to stop by each morning to pick up their day's credentials, we got on a first-name basis with many of them. No two days were ever alike or typical, but there were a few that were especially memorable.

HILL, ALFRE AND OTHERS

Shez (pronounced Shay) a volunteer from the L.A. Finance Office, and I were working the credentials window together. She knew just about everybody from L.A., and I knew most people from Chicago. We greeted folks, checked IDs, got signatures, and handed out credentials for entering the hotel, for getting into meeting rooms within the hotel, and gave instructions on where to pick up credentials for the next day's meetings and speeches at the Denver Convention Center and Pepsi Center. We were having a lot of fun laughing and joking with folks. Things were going well, so I decided to get a group picture of the credentials crew having a good time. As I stood outside of the credentials window, poised to take the snapshot, up walked Hill Harper, Alfre Woodard and another actress I recognized but couldn't call by name. I welcomed them to the convention. As they were getting their credentials verified, something told me to ask Hill if he'd mind taking a picture with me. Surprisingly, he said yes. I asked the actress whose name I didn't know if she'd take the picture, and she said yes. I put my arm around Hill's slim waist, and he put his arm around mine as he stood between Joyce and me and our big, happy smiles. The actress took the shot, and I thanked them both. Hill, Alfre, the actress lady, Shez and Joyce posed at the credentials window, and I took their picture. Once I got back on the other side of the counter, I handed the three of them a lanyard for their credentials. Hill shook my hand and told me that I had a beautiful smile. Alfre Woodard thanked me and mouthed that I had baby-soft, beautiful skin. I smiled and mouthed "thank you" back. I watched as they headed off to their rooms upstairs, and then looked down at the roster of names for that day's credentials. That's when I learned who the "actress lady" was: Kerry Washington, of "I Think I Love My Wife" fame. I hadn't yet seen the movie, but I knew that I'd seen her face. I thought *how nervy of me* to ask *her* to take a picture of *me*. And how humble of her to simply say, "Yes" and do it.

ॐ

Over the course of the following days, I saw, smiled at, interacted with, and even got pictures with so many high-profile names and famous faces until it nearly made me light-headed. Of all of them, the following encounters were especially memorable:

- A frustrated Chris Kofinis, former Communications Director for the John Edwards campaign, none too pleased at hearing,

"No, sorry Mr. Kofinis. We don't have you on our credentials list";

- Donna Brazille, Vice President Al Gore's 2000 campaign manager, author and political analyst for CNN, chatting it up in the lobby of the Hyatt Hotel with Suzanne Malveaux's cousin, Dr. Julianne Malveaux, economist, political commentator and president of Bennett College;
- Harold Ford, Jr., former U. S. Representative from Tennessee, laughing and talking to a small knot of folks, including Douglas Wilder, former governor of Virginia, who was being embraced by a well-wisher;
- James Carville, 1992 campaign manager for President Bill Clinton, who flashed an impish smile on the other side of the glass door of the revolving doors that we shared;
- A talkative Judge Mathis, laughing and having a fun time with friends as we passed each other on the street. I smiled. He was too busy talking to notice;
- The day I garnered close-up shots of me and Chris Hughes, the Facebook cofounder who had recommended me for the GFC campaign video clip; and another one later that evening as I walked through downtown Denver and spotted Roland Burris, former Illinois comptroller and one of my public administration professors at Roosevelt University during my pursuit of a master's degree, and who was later appointed to replace Obama as Senator from Illinois;
- Riding the up escalator, passing Brit Hume, Fox News Network anchor, as he rode down; and later riding the down escalator, smiling and waving at Blair Underwood, who smiled and waved back as he rode up;
- Among a crowd of thousands waiting outside in the security check line of the Pepsi Center, underneath a clean, blue sky and mellow sun, ahead in line by a few hundred of a shaded Angela Bassett, Spike Lee and his wife Tonya;
- Nearly missing spotting House Speaker Nancy Pelosi outside of

the Pepsi Center as she walked past, well guarded by a diamond-shaped security team surrounding her, and as usual, dressed to the hilt in a baby blue silk skirt suit, off-white pumps and pearls;

- Walking the massive hallways of the Pepsi Center, en route to hear the night's featured speakers, passing the likes of California Congresswoman Maxine Waters holding court with a clump of intent listeners; or speaking to New York Congressman Charles Rangel, chairman of the powerful House Ways and Means Committee, who smiled, winked and spoke in return;

- And witnessing the process of ad hoc hotel lockdowns at the Westin whenever one of the Obamas or any of the former presidents and first ladies returned to or departed from the hotel. Literally, the hotel doors were locked on one side so that no one could enter or leave while the Secret Service guarded them; while the Denver police, dressed in full riot gear of helmets with drop-down face shields, guns and knee pads lined the street opposite the unlocked doors; then came the motorcade led by two police cars with flashing red and blue lights, closely followed by several black SUVs with smoked windows, making it impossible for anyone to know which SUV carried Michelle or Barack Obama, Bill or Hillary Clinton, Joe or Jill Biden, or Jimmy or Rosalynn Carter. You only knew that someone big was being transported in or out of the hotel. And as suddenly and ceremoniously as the caravan appeared, the contortion of cars equally as suddenly swerved into the underground garage and disappeared, leaving me smiling, my heart racing and feeling as happy as the kid I was running barefoot through the grassy fields of Greenville, Mississippi.

These memories rolled like waves in my mind, leaving an imprint with each tide and ebb, consuming the nightly rides back to the "host house" of my seventy-nine-year-old hostess, Mrs. Annie Walker. She and Sylvester, a loving couple, caught up in their own sweet world of playing cards (for a nickel a hand), drinking Paul Masson red wine, laughing, nudging each other, and in general being happy, punctuated the warm and happy feeling of my time spent in Denver. And as usual, at the end of each night after rolling my hair, washing off makeup, saying my prayers and thinking of James, I'd fall asleep to the sounds of their laughter and chorus of "I'll see your nickel and raise you a dime."

ço

THE SPEECHES
Michelle Obama

"Sweetie!" James answered his phone.

"Hey, Sweetie!"

"I'm watching Craig Robinson right now!"

"Yeah, well I'm watching Craig Robinson live!" I replied.

We both laughed before talking for just a quick minute. We knew Michelle would be up soon. We said our good-byes, my heart racing, feeling the joy and love through the cellular phone lines.

Just moments before, heading into the Pepsi Center, "the gang": Joyce, June, Judy, Yvonne and I, hopped the free shuttle from the hotel to the Pepsi Center dropoff. The weather was warm and sunny, with scents of grilled burgers, onions and beer flowing out from the CNN Grill as we passed by. A noisy commotion made us all suddenly turn. A rotund lady had tripped, snapping her index finger out of place as she tried to break the fall of her approximate 300 pounds. She let out a horrible cry, her finger bent backwards and entire body shaking in apparent pain. Those of us near stopped to help, pulling out cell phones and looking for police. Two young men came over, grabbed her hand, and popped the swollen finger back into place. I had 9-1-1 on the telephone explaining the situation, and yelling out asking if she wanted them to call for an ambulance. The young men, helping her to her feet, told her that they'd walk with her, and make sure she got inside the Pepsi Center. With that assurance, she shook her head "no" at me. She was crying and thanking us and seemed better as we all resumed our walk towards the arena. Sitting waiting for Michelle Obama to come onstage, I thought about the lady who had fallen – what determination. Even though they'd pulled her finger back into its proper place, she still must have been in incredible pain and yet didn't want to miss a moment of this history in the making. I wondered if she'd made it in. I looked around at the packed arena of tens of thousands of people, and wondered what sacrifice of life or limb they'd made to be there too.

I could see the speakers as they came from backstage. Michelle was entering, wearing a pretty but plain sea-foam-colored dress, minimal jewelry and hair flowing into a shoulder-length pageboy. She looked every bit the First Lady. I'd seen Michelle live a few times before and knew that she could be both elegant and fiery; the attorney and community activist; or the sister girl from the South Side one moment and the reassuring mom the next. Tonight she was the proud wife. She was a woman in love, filled with pride for her man. She was soft and elegant and talked about the delicate balancing act of being both a professional woman and a full-time mother; about how she met Barack and fell in love and came to marry him. She talked about the family values that she and Barack were raised on, and how they tried to instill those same values in their own girls. The theme of her speech was about their "improbable journey" and focused on the American dream of the possibility of becoming anything that your heart and mind desired, and of how she and Barack were a living example of this belief. She was gentle, sincere, passionate and touching. So that by the end of her speech, wherein a real expression of love for her husband, their children, her mother, her brother, and this country was so evident, the emotions of the crowd overflowed, as did the tears.

We gave her a standing ovation, waving flags and "Michelle" signs. Her daughters Malia and Sasha joined her onstage, and then suddenly Barack Obama appeared on the big screen via satellite. The arena filled with frantic whoops and hollers, and the night became fantastic. Afterwards, "the gang" hugged and high-fived as we prepared to reverse our steps to head home. Annie and Sylvester were waiting for me at the Westin. All the way home, we laughed and talked about the first night of the convention and Michelle's moving speech, our gleeful sounds flowing out the car windows into the cool night air, atop the urban noise of a city hosting a major political convention.

∽

HILLARY, BILL, AND JOE

Mrs. Walker was having a "watch party" on the night of Hillary Clinton's speech. I chose to stay and watch the speech from her place instead of seeing it live. I told myself it was because I was tired and needed to relax at home. The truth is, I was still angry at how hard and nasty Hillary had fought during the primary elections, and at how she and her supporters had threatened to challenge Obama's delegate count of 2,118 as being insufficient for the nomination. I also wanted to support Mrs. Walker, who was busy fixing hors d'oeuvres platters and punch. Nine people from her neighborhood came out to watch the speech and do some phone-banking. Afterwards, we ate lunchmeat and crackers, raw veggies and deviled eggs. We kicked back and listened in on the speeches. Hillary was next.

"No way. No how. No McCain!"

That was her mantra throughout the speech. It was powerful and what Obama supporters needed to hear. Like her or not, she was feisty and knew how to boil a message down to a hard hitting sound-bite. She looked magnificent, too, in an orange silk pant suit that radiated her skin and made her look well rested. She started speaking in a slow wind-up and ended with knocking her message of Democratic Party unity out of the ballpark. The small lump of women in Mrs. Walker's basement were smiling and clapping at the conclusion of her speech. She'd won back our support. I thought about the DNC staff's rundown of one of the purposes of the convention: *to unify the party*. She'd done that, and we were proud of her.

The next evening, President Bill Clinton and vice-presidential nominee Joe Biden were scheduled to speak at the Pepsi Center. By noon things were rolling along relatively smoothly at the credentials office. We worked the credentials window, smiling, laughing, charming the guests as we got signatures and issued badges to the night's prized event. Excitement and anticipation filled the air and our moods. By the afternoon, we were famished and savored the lunch choices of albacore tuna on dark rye with potato salad, or turkey wraps with Greek salads, or roast beef on wheat with chips and pasta salad, each served with our choice of water, coffee, sodas or juice. I slowly consumed a smoky-flavored tuna sandwich washed down by a sparkling blackberry soda, as I wondered with each bite about our chances of scoring tickets for the night.

"Yeah, baby!" We shouted, after Bridget gave us credentials for the night's speeches.

"My man, Joe," I smiled and said to Shez.

"My man, Bill," she responded with a sly wink.

The center was filled to the hilt. It seemed as if every Democrat in Denver wanted to hear President Clinton and Joe Biden. The seats we had for the night's event were not the best – high up and nearly behind the stage. We didn't care. We were there live, inside the Pepsi Center, among hordes of Democratic prominence. The lights dimmed. The music revved up. President Clinton stepped out from the shadows backstage and into the spotlight. We jumped to our feet, yelling and clapping and waving small American flags. He kept saying "thank you, thank you" as he indicated for us to take our seats. We wouldn't. We shouted, "We love you!" He graciously smiled and said, "Thank you." The ovation, hoots and hollers continued. Again, he attempted to start his speech, but we wouldn't let him. We stood and clapped and wanted him to know that although we loved Obama, we loved him too. We wanted him to know that we forgave him for his "fairy tale" comment during the South Carolina primary and for his overall below-the-belt actions during the rough-and-tumble contest between Obama and his wife. We stood and clapped and yelled for over a full minute. He stood there in humble submission and absorbed the outpouring of love.

He started to speak again. This time we let him.

"Thank you. Thank you so much! You know, I – I love this, and I thank you, but we have important work to do tonight. I am here first to support Barack Obama."

An explosion of applause ensued at the mention of Barack Obama's name. President Clinton continued.

"And second – and, second, I'm here to warm up the crowd for Joe Biden. Though, as you will soon see, he doesn't need any help from me."

Another explosion of applause ensued at the mention of Joe Biden's name too.

"I love Joe Biden, and America will, too!"

The crowd erupted again and gradually settled down as President Clinton began talking about why he was supporting Obama: because Obama was a man who inspired and who inspired sound policies; because of his great grasp of foreign policy and national security; and because coupled with Joe Biden's tenured experience and wisdom, America would have a formidable national security team; and lastly, because Barack Obama was "ready to be President of the United States!"[23]

We jumped to our feet again, clapping and shouting. Just as his wife had done the night before, President Clinton had also hit a home run. Clinton finished his speech and turned the stage over to Joe Biden's oldest son, Beau. And after a warm introduction of his father, Joe Biden took the stage. With music piped in and the crowd cheering, Joe Biden approached the podium and gave us that brilliant smile of his that forces his left eye to wink in the process.

"Thank you very much. You know, folks, my dad used to have an expression. He'd say, 'A father knows he's a success when he turns and looks at his son or daughter and knows that they turned out better than he did.' I'm a success. I'm a helluva success. Beau, I love you, I'm so proud of you. I'm so proud of the son you've become; I'm so proud of the father you are.

"And I am truly honored – I am truly honored to live in a country with the bravest warriors in the world. And I'm honored to represent the first state, my state, the state of Delaware.

"Since I've never been called a man of few words, let me say this as simply as I can: Yes. Yes, I accept your nomination to run and serve with Barack Obama, the next president of the United States of America!"[24]

---

[23] Excerpts from the transcript "Bill Clinton Convention Speech," *New York Times*, August 27, 2008 – U.S./Politics [http://www.nytimes.com/2008/08/27/us/politics/27text-clinton.html].

[24] Excerpts from the transcript "Joseph R. Biden's Convention Speech," *New York Times*, August 27, 2008 – U. S./Politics [http://www.nytimes.com/2008/08/27/us/politics/27text-biden.html].

Joe Biden went on to give a short, sweet and sincere speech. And the audience reacted in kind with applause, praise and sentiments of "I love you."

The night had been moving and magical and patriotic. Riding home, I reflected on my incredible day and the wonderful people I'd encountered: Obama's Harvard Law School classmate, Cassandra Butts; television judge, the Honorable Glenda Hatchett; 14th Ward Alderman Edward Burke of Chicago; Joe Biden's son; and I even got a glimpse of the fast-moving powerhouse Rahm Emmanuel. I smiled at the remembrances of the day and the uplifting words in the speeches. I'd come a long way with the campaign and now sat at the cusp of the most historic nomination yet. The warmth of these thoughts enveloped me like a sweet hug or kiss or the soothing dry air of the night breeze. I held them closely as I looked out the car window into the blackness of the night, and anticipated the next day – the nomination of Barack Obama, an African American and the Democratic Party's nominee for president.

INVESCO FIELD

Nabbing Tickets to Get In

This was the day we'd waited on for eight months, since the win in Iowa and loss in New Hampshire; since the fervor over Reverend Wright and the calm of the Race Speech; since the left-wing outcry against the FISA bill; since the bowling debacle, and all of the other ups and downs of the campaign, this was the historic moment for which we'd waited.

I awoke early that morning. The soft Denver sun played peek-a-boo through the cracks of the mini-blinds. I sprang from the bed and said my morning prayers. *Thank you Father, for bringing us this far. I pray for a safe, successful and joyous day. Amen.*

I took the clothes that I would wear from the closet: black stretch jeans, white tuxedo shirt, black silk belt with a crystal buckle. I rubbed the breast of the shirt. It belonged to James. It was the shirt he wore when his band had to dress in full formal gear. It was important to him, so it was important to me. He'd wanted me to have something of his that I could take on the trip to Denver, that I could take to Invesco Field so that a piece of him could share in the historic moment. I wished he was there in the flesh. I rubbed the hem and tail of the shirt as if summoning strength from the fabric that belonged to him. Throughout this entire journey, he had been there encouraging me on. He had become a great source of strength for me. I looked at the shirt and smiled. *Good morning, Sweetie*, I thought. *I miss you and wish you were here.*

৬

"Good morning, Judge Hatchett!" I said brightly.

"Well, good morning to you, Michelle," she responded, shaking my hand across the credentials booth counter.

"Today's the day, huh? Are you excited?" I asked, scanning the roster for her name.

"You better believe I am."

"Here's your credential for the speech tonight. Nice section. Good seat."

"Good. Hmm, let's see. Oh, this is in a different section from my friend. Can you get us together in her section, Michelle?"

"Sure. Let's have her ticket," I said reaching for her credential, not certain of whether I could get them together or not.

Judge Hatchett turned and beckoned her friend over. And none other than Dr. Johnnetta Cole, first African American woman president of Spelman College, stepped forward.

"Michelle, this is my friend, Johnnetta Cole." Judge Hatchett said.

"Oh, yes ma'am. I know exactly who you are, Dr. Cole," I said, looking at her. "I attended Clark Atlanta University during your tenure at Spelman. It's a pleasure to meet you!" I beamed while shaking her hand.

I grabbed their two mix-matched credentials and without consulting Bridget or Joyce or anyone looked through the box of credentials for two seats that were together. I knew technically I should have asked, but for these two women I was willing to live up to the old adage of "I'd rather ask forgiveness rather than get permission." I also knew that as the "diplomat" of the group, I had been given certain license to make situations work. I swapped out the old credentials for two new ones.

"Here you go, ladies," I said, handing each of them a credential. "If I don't see you, enjoy the event tonight! It sure was a pleasure meeting you both."

"No, the pleasure has been all mine. You have really helped me. If there's anything I can ever do for you, let me know," Judge Hatchett said, gently squeezing my hand.

I smiled, started to speak and hesitated. They turned to leave and I clumsily asked, "Uh, excuse me, Judge Hatchett. Would you mind if I got a picture of you both?"

"Honey, I'll do you one better. How about you take a picture with the both of us!" she said through perfectly white teeth and a warm smile.

So we did. Time stood still for the moment that Judge Glenda Hatchett, Dr. Johnnetta Cole and I embraced, smiled and archived that moment of that historic day.

That's how the day began, in stark contrast to the day before of missing credentials, in which Judge Hatchett had gotten entangled. Everyone on both sides of the credentials booth was in high spirits. The line was non-stop with people waiting to pick up the coveted Invesco Field ticket coated with holograms that toggled between a profile of Barack Obama and the American flag with the words "Barack Obama, Democratic Presidential Candidate, Thursday, August 28, 2008" engraved underneath. By the end of our four-hour shift, "the gang" had credentials as well. We were seated in the Floor Section, which meant we had nearly full access to the stadium, including the floor where the dignitaries and delegates sat. Our credentials also had something on them that I hadn't seen on others, a blue dot sticker at the top. The only explanation Bridget offered when she gave us the credentials was to "just act as if you belong there."

At the time, those words held no special meaning, and the blue dot was no more than a mere curiosity. The dot's significance became clear after I'd returned home to Chicago. Whether a blue dot, red dot, yellow dot, no dot, we cared not. We had credentials to see live the most historic speech of the campaign yet! We had an heirloom and oral history to pass down to our children and grandchildren, nephews and great-nieces. We had an item that was being sold on the underground market for upwards of $1,200. I clenched the credential, watching the holograms change from Obama to the flag. The five of us jumped up and down, yelling the same as we had done years before at high school football games. We did a group hug around Joyce, thanking her profusely for recommending us to be on the "Friends and Family" Credentials Team.

We gathered our things, walking shoes, cameras, purses, cell phones, bottled water and any other aids that got us through the day. I spotted Shez and her mother and friends.

"Hey, Shay!"

"Hi, Michelle!"

I leaned in close and quietly asked, "Did you get credentials for to-night?"

"Yeah," she said, showing me the same kind of blue-dotted credential that I had. "Girl, Bridget pulled these out from a secret stash!"

"They must be something special, huh?" I asked.

"Must be," Shez said with a hunch of her shoulders.

We hugged, smiled, said good-bye and swapped phone numbers before I ran off to catch up with the rest of the gang. We were headed outside to board the bus that was taking VIPs to Invesco Field. It was still hours before Obama was scheduled to speak, but the wait time to clear security, and get inside the stadium was projected to take between one to three hours. Over a million people had been projected to descend upon Denver on this day, and security was tight. We went downstairs and lined up behind the small group of people waiting to board the VIP bus.

"Sorry ma'am, can't let you through," the female security guard softly but firmly told Joyce.

"Whatcha mean?" Joyce queried. "We're part of the Credentials Team. We have clearance to board the bus," she demanded, stepping forward.

The security guard held up a stop-sign-like hand and repeated, "Sorry, can't let you on the bus. Not without a credential that looks like this."

The guard flashed a yellowish-gold credential stamped with the August 28, 2008 date and the words: *Invesco Field, VIP*.

Deflated, we moved out of the way of others behind us who did have the proper credentials. Shez, who had twisted her ankle a couple of days before, leaned on crutches. Her mom, somewhere between her late seventies and early eighties, looked both perplexed and childlike. Joyce wanted to cuss. I needed a smoke. June kept asking, "What's going on?" leaving Judy and Yvonne to only hunch their shoulders, indicating, "I dunno." We were a pretty sad-looking crew.

We turned and retraced our steps back inside the hotel and upstairs to the credentials office. Shez hobbled a good distance behind, with her mother at her side.

"Bridget, we couldn't get on the bus," Joyce said defiantly.

"Whatcha mean?"

"We couldn't get on," Joyce repeated. "We need some special credential. A yellowish-looking thing."

Bridget unlocked her desk drawer and fished around a bit. "Like these?" she asked.

"Yeah," Joyce said with a smile.

Our hearts collectively lifted as we waited for Bridget to issue us the bus passes. She pulled out two, closed the drawer and locked it again, saying, "Sorry ladies, this is all I have. I was told the credentials I gave you would get you on the bus and inside the stadium."

"Two credentials? That's all you've got? Bridget, there are five of us!" Joyce impatiently said, taking the credentials from Bridget.

"Seven," Shez corrected. "Me and my mom make seven."

"Seven. There are seven of us," Joyce corrected herself.

"Sorry ladies," Bridget responded. "It's the best I can do. Gotta go. They need me at the window. Sorry."

With that said, Bridget returned to the credentials counter. We stared at the two tickets and at one another, with that "what-us-gon'-do-now-Ms.-Celie?" look on our faces, the same as Nettie in the movie *The Color Purple* had whenever she and Celie faced trouble. Joyce broke the ice.

"Well, I say the oldest in the group get the bus passes. So, I think June and Shez's mom should ride the bus."

Shez's mom looked sadly at her daughter and then looked towards her daughter's busted ankle. Shez spoke up. "I can't ride a public bus and train and then walk to Invesco Field on these crutches. I just won't be able to make it."

"And I don't need to ride the bus," June protested. "I can take the train. I can walk if I have to!"

"Well, I heard that public trains and buses can't get within a mile of Invesco Field," Yvonne added.

"Yeah, I heard that too," Judy chimed in.

"Who among us think we can walk the mile?" I asked, raising my hand.

June and Yvonne raised theirs, too.

"You can't walk no mile, June! In this heat? At your age?" Joyce scolded.

"I beg your pardon. I exercise everyday, Joyce. I can make it. Humph!" June retorted. "If it's the last thing I do, I'm gonna be at Invesco Field tonight."

There was an awkward silence. Joyce, as we all did, sensed not to push June on this issue. June was right, although she was in her early eighties; she drank plenty of water and was as fit as a fiddle. Besides, we all knew that she had lost her husband about a month prior, and before he died they'd made a penny bet on whether they'd live to see a black man become president, or even see one be nominated for the high office. Her husband had bet that they wouldn't live long enough to see it happen, because that day was too far off in the distant future. June had bet that they would, because Obama was going to be the first black president and that day was just around the corner. She was determined to be at the stadium that night, to stand in the stead of her husband; to represent her family; to provide pictures and oral history to her granddaughters; to make good on her penny bet.

"Joyce, if June says she can make it, she can make it," Judy said.

"Yeah, and we can stop and rest along the way if we need to," I added.

"I don't need to rest. I need to move! Come on, let's get going!" June said. "Besides Joyce, you need the bus pass. You won't be able to walk that far with all of your knee problems."

"Girl, I've seen Barack speak live a hundred times. I don't have to go. I got my keepsake and I'm going back to our host house and watch the speech on a jumbotron they'll have set up. I don't need the bus pass."

"Well, that settles it," June said. "Looks like Shez and her mother should get the tickets."

Joyce scanned our faces for a moment and weighed the fairness of none of the Chicago crew getting to board the bus, so that Shez from Los Angeles could go. In her mind, somehow that scenario just didn't seem right.

"You ladies agree with that?" Joyce asked, looking dead on at us.

"Agreed," Yvonne said.

"Agreed," I said.

"Me, too," Judy added.

"Then let's go!" June said.

And so we did. We waved good-bye to Shez and her mother, and began our long journey to Invesco Field.

THE TREK TO THE STADIUM

Weather-wise, the day was beautiful – not too hot, not too cool. The temperature hovered in the upper seventies. As if smiling down on Denver, the sun was high and bright. Upper seventies in Denver felt more like a nice cool 70 degrees to my hot-and-humid-Chicago-weathered skin. June, Judy, Yvonne and I huddled for a moment to map a game plan for getting to the stadium. We knew we could only come within a mile before we'd have to walk, and we had three miles between us at the hotel and the stadium. We agreed on taking the free shuttle from the Westin to the end of the line at Union Station LoDo (Lower Downtown) and from there take the light rail public train as far in as we could. So we set out on our journey with the sun on our shoulders, smiles on our faces, wind in our hair, and prized credentials in our bags.

"End of the line folks! Everyone off, please," the shuttle driver announced. The shuttle was packed. In fact, three shuttles before were packed, but we'd pushed and squeezed our way onto this one. It was a relief to be off of the hot, tight bus and out into the fresh air. My beloved tuxedo shirt had gotten a bit rumpled and my hair disheveled from more than one elbow to the head. All in all, I was fine and had made it through the first leg of our journey.

"'Cuse me, sir," Yvonne said to a policeman. "Which way do we go to get on the light rail train to Invesco Field?"

"Trains aren't going there today, ma'am," the police officer said, wiping sweat from his brow.

"I know. How close can we get, though? You know, what stop do we get off?"

"Oh, about a couple stops in. You can probably get off at the Pepsi Center station. But good luck with that, though. You see that line over there?"

"Yes."

"That's the line to get into the train station."

"Whoa!" Yvonne exclaimed, looking over at the long lines of hundreds of people.

"Yeah, been queuing up for a couple of hours now," the officer said.

"Well, can we get a bus or cab or something that'll get us close to the stadium?"

"You can try," the officer said with a note of exasperation and another wipe of the brow. "Try the number 32 at 15th and Blake Street. Good luck."

Luck and prayers were what we needed. In order to get the number 32, we'd need to get back on the shuttle bus and take it back down the mall to get to Blake Street. And as we'd just experienced, the buses were packed. Our options were running out, and we still had over two miles between us and the stadium.

"Let's get a cab," Judy suggested.

"To where?" I asked.

"As close to the stadium as it will take us."

"Well, how much will that cost us?"

"Yeah, Judy, that can get expensive," June chimed in.

"And the cabs are probably full, too," Yvonne added with a sigh.

"Just a suggestion, ladies," Judy conceded.

The area where we stood was beginning to get crowded, and the police officer egged us to move along. Confounded about which way to go to get to the stadium, we simultaneously began to move and decided that we'd walk south towards the stadium and hail a cab en route.

We tried hailing several dozen cabs. They didn't stop because they were all full. We saw bicycle rickshaws and tried hailing them. They were all full, too. So we continued to walk. People were walking in all directions, zigzagging across the streets, some seeming determined to get to their destination and walking with a hard, purposeful stride; some seeming to stroll casually; others laughing and talking as they walked; while others, like us, looked lost. We weren't completely lost. We just didn't know the exact route to take to the stadium. We had no street maps, MapQuest or Yahoo directions. We just knew that the stadium was due south, and that was the direction that most of the people seemed to be headed. Giving up, for the moment, on finding an available cab, we walked along Wynkoop Street to 14th Street to Blake Street and followed its contours as it curved to the right, then left, then right again. The sun was beginning to pierce my cotton shirt, and the tag in the back was nipping my neck. I adjusted the shoulder strap of my purse, tried to undo the top button of the shirt, but the hole was too tight. The trip was just beginning, with only about thirty minutes in, and I was beginning to fade. My silver and onyx sandals, while cute, were not a wise decision for walking three miles on warm concrete sidewalks.

"Keep your eyes out for a cab, ladies," Yvonne instructed.

"Okay," Someone from the pack responded.

I thought for a moment about how if I was beginning to feel the weight of my purse and the trip ahead of us, just how much more intense it must be for the rest of the gang. At nearly fifty years old, I was the junior of the group. Everyone else was retired and in their golden years, with Judy in her late sixties and June in her early eighties. *Lord, help us,* I prayed.

Judy was beginning to look a bit fatigued, her long blonde hair starting to curl at her temples and neck where she sweated. We passed several taverns and restaurants along the winding avenue and decided to stop in one to load up on water and sugary snacks. We came out and spotted a cab.

"Hey! Taxi!" we yelled.

The yellow SUV-like vehicle stopped.

"Can you take us as close to Invesco Field as possible?" Yvonne asked the cabbie.

"Well, they got the streets cut off so bad 'til it'll be better for me to take you where they have shuttles that'll take you close to the stadium."

"They got shuttles going to the stadium?" we asked in near unison.

"Yeah. You got tickets to get in?"

"Yes."

"Well, them tickets'll get you on the shuttle," the cabbie said reassuringly.

"Cool! All right then," we said.

We loaded into the cab. He rounded the corner and drove less than a half mile before pulling into a large lot lined with coach buses.

"Here we are ladies. That'll be $12.50."

"This is it?" I asked. "We weren't that far away," I said, fishing through my purse to pony up my portion of the fare.

"Not far, but we wouldn't have found it on our own," Judy answered.

"True," I said as we thanked and paid the driver.

He waved, folding the ten and five into his front breast pocket as he pulled off.

"Is this the bus to Invesco Field?" June asked.

"Yes, Ma'am. Are you with the Rand Corporation?" the driver asked pleasantly.

"No, sir."

"Sorry, this is a charter for the Rand Corporation."

"Are there any buses for the general public?"

"Hmm, not sure. You ladies may want to check with the office over there."

"Thanks," we grumbled as we unhuddled from around the bus driver.

"Hi, officer. Which of these buses are for the general public?"

"Oh, they're up the road a piece, near the regular bus stop," the officer responded, pointing southward. "Just stay on this sidewalk and follow the curve around. You'll see 'em about a couple of blocks down."

"Thanks," we grumbled again.

My forehead, temples and back were sweating. I fanned the tail of the shirt to allow some air to bellow in. The shirt tag scratched my neck, making me stop fanning the shirt. I returned to sweating. We followed the officer's instructions and followed the sidewalk around the curves of what seemed to be an office park. The unsettling part about being in a place of which you're not familiar is that totally helpless feeling of always being on the verge of being lost. I felt it. I'm sure the rest of the gang felt it too. But we pressed on, looking for a group of buses near the "regular" bus stop.

"There they are!" I yelled, pointing towards a line of black and gray coach buses.

We picked up our stride and approached the chariots that awaited us.

"Need to see your credentials, please," a stout, uniformed driver said.

"Yes, sir," we said, happily pulling out our prized Invesco tickets.

The driver crinkled his nose and shook his head at the sight of the tickets. "No, I mean the green credentials. Ya know, ta enter the bus."

"What green credentials?" June impatiently asked.

"The green ones. Like this," the driver said dryly as he held up a kelly-green credential stamped *transportation – general public.*

"Well, we don't have that. We only have the Invesco passes," Judy said.

"Sorry. Can't let ya on without 'em."

"Well, where can we get some?" Judy pressed.

"Can't. Not now. They're all gone. Sold out in minutes. Sorry, ladies," the driver said as he waved forward a group of people with the proper credentials.

"Well, what do we do now?" Judy asked of no one in particular.

We stared back blankly.

"Walking's the only way left, ladies," the driver responded. "I wouldn't recommend it, though. That'll be some hike from here to the Field."

"Well, what other option do we have?" I asked.

The driver hunched his shoulders and responded, "Dunno."

The space between us and Invesco Field was still roughly two miles. Not bad in a vehicle, hard as hell though on foot during the high sun. With fallen spirits, moist makeup and curling hair against the dry heat, we steeled our backs and braced for the long walk ahead of us. One foot in front of the other, one hunched, hot, sweaty step at a time, we walked. We walked alongside other clumps of people whose options had also run out; alongside young men in dreadlocks with little children on their shoulders whose small feet dangled against their chests; alongside old white men with chest-length beards and tight tee-shirts over fat stomachs; alongside bright-eyed idealists with youth and frivolity on their sides; alongside the disabled aided by wheelchair pushers and walking canes; over camel-back pedestrian overpasses with snarled highway traffic underneath; one foot in front of the other, one step at a time until my sandal straps pinched and ball-of-the-feet calluses hurt; until Judy, quite out of breath, panted, "Stop."

It was eighty-something-year-old June we'd been concerned about, but it was Judy who was withering the fastest. Her skin had become clammy, and her hair had turned into a damp blonde mop in the back. We rested against the railings of the overpass and drank bottled water, rested our shoulder bags and rubbed our feet.

"You all right?" Yvonne asked Judy after a while.

"Yeah, thanks," she responded in a more normal cadence.

"Man, I feel like we're crossing through the Underground Railroad or something," Yvonne said more to herself than to anyone else.

"Yeah, well what would Harriet Tubman have done in this situation?" I asked. She'd put one foot in front of the other and push against those ahead of her and say, "Just keeping moving. When you hear the dogs, just keep moving. When you hear the sheriffs, just keep moving. I know it hurts, but keep moving. I know you're tired and hungry, but keep moving. We're almost there, just keep moving."

And that became our chant, when any of us got tired or needed a break to rest. "Just keep moving," is what we told ourselves to move forward.

Near the end of the trail, a few hundred feet before the mile-wide security perimeter, we'd come to a literal crossroad. Wooden traffic horses blocked the intersection of the Y-shaped streets. Traffic cops guided the motorized traffic, while beat cops directed those of us on foot. Most of the pedestrian traffic was herded to the right of the Y-shaped street and onto the walkways that led to the front of Invesco Field. We, along with a few others, were splintered from the herd and directed towards a "short cut" which led us to the back of the field. The cop's directions had been to turn left, go over a rolling hill and we'd see the back of the field on the other side. The parts he left out were the crumbling gravel and dirt and rocks underfoot on the steep climb down the other side of the rolling hill.

June was in trouble. Strong as she may have been, her knees and thighs couldn't maneuver the steeply angled slope. It required a strong back and thighs and deep knee bends to maintain a balance against the pull of gravity. Without question or request for help from June, Yvonne and I each locked arms around June's tiny waist with our shoulders propped against her underarms until her feet were raised slightly off the ground. With carefully choreographed baby-steps, we carried June down the hill, through the steepness, through the biting rocks and tumbleweed bristles. For about a three-minute, stooped, duck-like walk, we descended the side of the hill. The weight of gravity pulled at my knees and legs and strained my back. Sweat rolled freely down the sides of my face, breast cleavage and seam of my back. The embroidered shirt tag felt like sandpaper eating through my skin with each tug of my shirt sleeve. *Just keep moving*, I told myself. *We're almost there. Just keep moving.*

THE ACCEPTANCE SPEECH

My legs were water, like unsteady streams of tiredness. Despite that, I felt joy. We'd made it inside the stadium. The trek had been long and hard, but once inside the cool underbelly of the arena that buzzed with anxious and happy people, the journey had also been worth it. I looked over at June. She looked like a precious, tiny, collectible doll whose porcelain had become just a bit cracked over time, which gave it value and character. She had weathered the journey just fine. She stood staring up towards the exposed ceiling and just beamed with pride. Perhaps she was praying, perhaps talking silently to her late husband. She didn't know it, but I'd drawn as much emotional strength from her as she had leaning on our physical might and muscle.

"Ain't this wonderful, June?" I asked.

"It's a blessing, girl. That's what it is."

And she was right. We were blessed to be there live and with good seats to experience history first-hand.

"What are we waiting for?" Yvonne interrupted. "Let's get to our seats!"

We walked the inclining pathway that led us from underneath the stadium and up to the stands. The roar of the crowd got louder the higher up we went. Scores of people were there already, tens of thousands, with a crowd of nearly 80,000 expected to fill the place. The excitement was palpable. My heart began to race. I was no longer a weary tired, but a joyful tired, the kind of muscle-aching tired after tending a garden all day. Smells of tap beer, and hotdogs and pretzel dough on the rotisseries followed us as we ascended the staircase to the "Floor Level." We stepped out into the open arena. In a word, it was magnificent. We walked in on an organic symphony of singing and laughter and talking and drum beats and smiles and cameras and children posing and women giggling and men high-fiving and America coming together as a pride-filled nation awaiting a moment in history that none of us would ever forget. And at each turn, my eyes captured separate, personal stories being told, like a camera clicking and saving the images in my mind's eye.

We waded through the crowds of people wandering about, walking to and fro, until we descended into the pit-like Floor Level where the state delegates and news personnel were assigned.

"Let's look for seats numbered in the nineties," Yvonne suggested, as she took the lead in walking through the crowd.

It was crowded and tight and nice. I didn't mind one bit the literal rubbing shoulders with prominent politicians, pundits, newscasters, sports celebrities and the like. The sun and the cool, dry air hugged us as a soft breeze blew down. We walked past Franco Harris, of Pittsburgh Steelers fame, and nodded. He smiled. We shook hands with Emil Jones, former president of the Illinois Senate. I took snapshots of civil rights great Congressman John Lewis; women's rights attorney Gloria Allred; Illinois Congressman Jesse Jackson, Jr.; and MSNBC political analyst Richard Wolffe. Although our credential passes contained seat numbers, there were no numbered seats on the Floor Level, so we circled the floor a couple of times and decided to just grab a clump of seats that would accommodate the four of us.

We had nearly two hours to kill before Obama would take the stage. So we sat back and rocked along with the crowd as the music carried us through the evening. I looked around and just inhaled the sights. The mile-high stadium had been transformed into a colossal replica of classical Greco-Roman architecture, with ornate Corinthian columns and velvety navy drapes flanking the center stage. Jumbotrons were in place in all directions. Stevie Wonder was performing on the actual stage, with his image multiplied on the high screens to the east and west of us. The clarity of the surround-sound PA system defiantly lifted the music above the chatter of the crowd. My heart was beating in rhythm with the bass drum. The crowd and I, with bobbing heads and swaying shoulders, sang along with Stevie Wonder: *"...here I am, signed, sealed, delivered. I'm yours!"*

I was feeling good. We all were. I fished my cell phone out of my bag and dialed James.

"Hey, Baby!" he said excitedly.

"Hey, Sweetie! We're here – at Invesco Field! We're here!"

"I'm watching it on TV! Is it as great as it seems?"

"Better! The music is literally rocking us. It's great! I'm wearing the shirt!"

"Cool," he said with pride.

"Yeah, so a piece of you is here with me."

"Real cool."

"I miss you, Sweetie."

"I miss you, too. Enjoy tonight. Take plenty of pictures and have a safe trip home."

"I will."

And I did.

The rest of the night was nothing less than magical. Speaker after speaker was fired up and inspiring, none more so than Barack Obama. A cloak of dusk was gently enveloping the stadium. We knew Obama was up next. We began stomping our feet in frenzied anticipation. When he stepped out onto the stage, an explosion of cheers and applause erupted. All of us there had waited so long for this moment; through miles of walking and hours of waiting in lines to get in; through week-long smiles and negotiations that smoothed away any credentials hiccups that had occurred; through months of answering phone calls at the national head-quarters; through knocking on doors and walking the streets of Iowa, Indiana, and other states across the nation. The anticipation of this moment was akin to the built-up passion of estranged lovers on the cusp of a rendezvous; a buildup so intense until it simply exploded at the sight of him. Then when he spoke, a heavy hush blanketed the arena.

"Four years ago, I stood before you and told you my story, of the brief union between a young man from Kenya and a young woman from Kansas who weren't well off or well known, but shared a belief that in America their son could achieve whatever he put his mind to.

"It is that promise that's always set this country apart, that through hard work and sacrifice each of us can pursue our individual dreams, but still come together as one American family, to ensure that the next generation can pursue their dreams, as well. That's why I stand here tonight."

The crowd interrupted the speech with applause.

". . .America, we are better than these last eight years. We are a better country than this. . . Tonight, tonight, I say to the people of America, to Democrats and Republicans and independents across this great land: Enough!"

The crowd erupted with applause again. And on and on, for the rest of the speech, the crowd peppered his words with brisk applause and cheers.

"America, we cannot turn back. We cannot walk alone.

"At this moment, in this election, we must pledge once more to march into the future. Let us keep that promise, that American promise, and in the words of scripture hold firmly, without wavering, to the hope that we confess.

"Thank you. God bless you. And God bless the United States of America."[25]

A full standing ovation was in progress by the time Obama finished his speech and his wife and children and the Bidens joined him onstage. He'd said what we'd come to hear. He'd accepted the nomination and inspired us to keep working for him to win the general election in November. We were standing and clapping, chanting, "Yes We Can!" to show our love and belief in his campaign. And suddenly a loud boom and crackle sounded off overhead, followed by a waft of gunpowder. My first thought was, *Oh God, gunshots!"* Fireworks, not gunshots, were sounding off like cannons, spewing colorful blasts of red, white, blue and gold streams of fire. The pyrotechnic display was high overhead and spectacular. The sound blasts were thunderous, the colors brilliant, a perfect punctuation to a week chocked with moving events. We all stood there, looking up with deep bends of the neck, watching the fiery performance, waving American flags and swaying to the sounds of Brooks and Dunn's *"Only in America"* cowboy tune. We basked in those moments of hyperbolic patriotism, loving every delicious moment.

I panned the crowd and felt the joy all around us. My heart pounded with each "kaboom" of the fire cannons. But when the red, white and blue streamers burst from above, descending onto the shoulders and heads of the Obamas and their little girls, and onto the Bidens and the people near the stage, streams of tears rolled down the faces of many of the people in the crowd as well. I looked around and witnessed grown men crying, little children crying; I was crying and so was June. Her husband had made it to see a black man get nominated for president of the United States after all, there in the person of her. I grabbed her hand and squeezed it. She smiled through the tears as we soaked in the last acts of the fireworks show. I held onto her hand and thought about how

[25] Excerpts from the transcript "Barack Obama's Speech at the Democratic National Convention," *New York Times*, August 28, 2008 – U.S./Elections [http://elections.nytimes.com/ 2008/president/conventions/videos/20080828_OBAMA_SPEECH.html#].

this crowd symbolized what the Obama campaign stood for – a mish-mash of people of all sizes, ages, shapes, colors and religious beliefs who, except for this one man, may not have otherwise ever met, who because of this one man had achieved something historical.

The Meltdown the Morning After

The morning after the speech at Invesco Field, I'd made it back home and was standing at the kitchen sink looking out over the backyard. Enjoying the sweet, hazelnut flavor of my first cup of coffee, I smiled – at nothing in particular and at everything all at once. I was happy. My cell phone rang. It was Shez from Los Angeles. One sound of her voice, and suddenly my mood changed.

"Hey Shay!" I squealed into the telephone. "What's up, girl?"

"Wh-where w-were y-you?" she asked in gasps.

"Whatcha mean?"

"Wh-where were you la-last night? At Invesco Field!" She practically screamed.

"I was with June 'nem, in the floor section."

"Wh-why, why weren't you in the section reserved for us?" she asked through tears.

"I don't know what you mean."

"The credentials that Bridget gave us. They were passes to the section with the Obama family and friends," she explained.

"What!" I exclaimed.

"Yes! I sat there waiting and looking for you. I sat right next to the Biden's daughter, right behind Michelle Obama. You hear me? Michelle Obama! Bridget and everybody were there. We were even on TV!"

"I, we, didn't know how to get to our seats," I responded. "We looked for them, but didn't see seats in the nineties."

"The dot, remember the little blue dot on the credential?"

"Yeah?"

"Well, that's what would have gotten you inside – gotten you inside the area where the friends and family were. I'm so sorry. I looked for you and waited. I didn't have your phone number on me or I woulda called you. Didn't Bridget tell you what the blue dot meant?"

"No. She didn't," I responded sadly, remembering that she'd only told us to *"act as if we belonged there."*

"Oh. I'm sorry," Shez said before hanging up.

Shez's revelation of the true value of the credentials we'd been given was knee-buckling. Without warning, I began to cry, hard. My hands began to shake. A nauseating sickness worked its way through my whole body. I sat down in a kitchen chair and bawled like a baby. And I couldn't explain why.

"You all right, Chelle?" Mom asked with great worry on her face.

"Ye – Yeah," I answered through chops of crying. "I – I'll be okay."

"Well, why're you crying?"

"I dunno. I just am."

She'd heard that answer enough over the years to know that now was not the time to press for an answer. She turned and went back upstairs, probably to pray for her daughter who was seemingly having a nervous breakdown. I worked my way down to the basement, where it was cool and quiet. I needed a smoke. I needed to stop crying. I needed to talk to my sister, Debra.

"H – Hi, Debbie," I slurred into the phone.

"Hey, Chelle. What's the matter?" she exclaimed. "Somebody do something to you?" she demanded in a big-sister voice.

"N – No, no. I – I just got back from Denver. A – And I'm having a meltdown."

"Something happen out there? I thought you were enjoying it."

"I – I was. I did. I can't explain why I'm crying. I just needed to talk to ya."

"Okay, girl. Take your time. Cry all you want. Talk when you're ready."

We held the telephone in silence, not a dead silence, but a patient one. A silence filled with love, with one sister channeling strength to the other. After a while, I started relaying the story that Shez had told me about the blue dot on the credential, about how I'd missed out on the opportunity to sit in the "friends and family" section of the arena. I told her about how Shez and her mother got separated from the rest of the gang, how we had to walk to the arena, helping June down the steep hill and through the brush.

"Wait a minute. Y'all helped the eighty-year-old sista make the trip? Got her down that hill?" Debbie interrupted.

"Yeah."

"Oooh, Chelle. Don't you see, girl. God placed you where you were most needed. You didn't need to be in no seat next to Michelle Obama. You've been blessed to be with her a few times. God used you and the rest of those sistas to help June to get into that stadium. D – Don't you see th – that? I'm so pr –proud of you I don't know what to do. You helped that poor sista live her dr – dream. . . ."

Her voice broke off. She was crying soft tears of sisterly pride. I'd stopped crying and felt better, too. I hadn't put my experience into a spiritual context, but leave it to Debbie to bring it all home for me. We ended our call on a happy note, with me recounting the many stories and antics and fireworks that had taken place during my week-long trip to Denver. I felt well enough to go talk to my mother, to explain that I'd been overcome with fatigue and a bit of sadness about not being in my assigned seat in the arena. I told her how Debbie had helped me to see that I was really in the right place after all. She agreed and beamed with a motherly pride of raising good daughters.

A little later, I felt well enough to call James, to share with him all that had happened since my morning call from Shez.

"Well, Michelle, don't you see? You weren't having a meltdown, Sweetie. You were going through a reconciliation of feelings and of times. Like some sort of parallel universe, you walked through living history in real time. You were living the 'past' as it was actually happening."

"You think so?"

"Yeah! The call from your friend made it click for you, that you all had just walked through history. And I agree with Debbie. You were in the right place doing the right thing with June. I'm proud of you too, Sweetie."

We ended our call and I felt much better. James could always do that for me. He somehow always knew the exact right thing to say. I lay down on the basement couch, feeling the soft breeze of the fan cool the August air. I lay there thinking, remembering, recalling the past recent events until sleep overcame me. I slept for twelve hours and awoke refreshed and refueled, ready for the next step of the campaign.

❧

"DNC CONVENTION – DENVER, COLORADO"

Other volunteers from Illinois along with Sylvester and Mrs. Annie Walker.

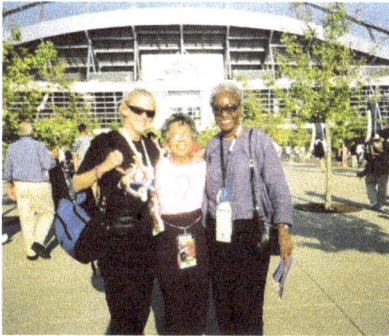

Mrs. Annie Walker, who provided my housing and transportation during my stay in Denver.

"The Gang," Judy, June and Yvonne after the long trek to Invesco Field for Barack Obama's acceptance speech as the Democratic nominee for president, August 28, 2008.

The Illinois Delegation

Me, all smiles sitting near the press booth.

Me and Chris Hughes, Co-founder of Face Book, at Westin Hotel during convention.

"DNC Convention – The Celebrities"

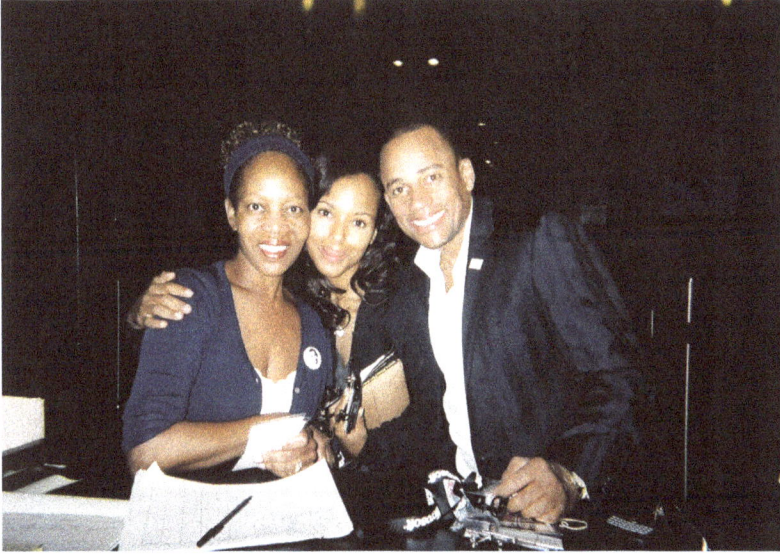

Alfre Woodard, Kerry Washington and Hill Harper after checking in at the "Friends & Family" credentials window.

Picture that Kerry Washington took of Joyce, Hill Harper and me at the credentials check-in window.

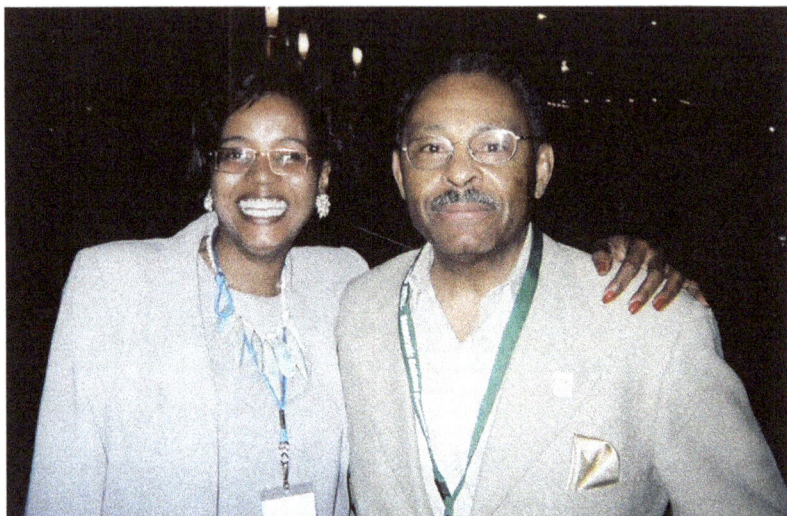

Me and Former U.S. Senator, Illinois 2nd Congressional District, Roland Burris in downtown Denver.

Sharing a moment with noted author, Walter Mosley, at the Westin Hotel during the DNC convention.

All smiles with Judge Glenda Hatchett of the Atlanta-based "Judge Hatchett Show."

Newscasters and politicians waiting for nominee, Barack Obama, to take center stage.

November 4, 2008

Dear Journal,

It's been a while since I've written, and a lot has happened. The campaign has revved up to execute a 50-state strategy in an effort to turn red and purple states blue. We're using a spoke-and-wheel model, with one central state being responsible for canvassing and campaigning in five surrounding states. Illinois is at the center of the wheel for the Midwest. We're responsible for assisting in Indiana, Iowa, Michigan, Missouri and Wisconsin. My friends and I have worked in Fishers, Indianapolis and Gary, Indiana. A small band of us have committed to canvassing in Gary, Indiana every weekend. I've recruited several people to be a part of that effort, including Cheryl Douthard and her family; Denise and her husband Mike, as well as her nephew Marc Whitfield; Don Baird and Todd Heldt from work; and of course, James. During our canvassing in Gary, Don and I met a college kid name Francis Motycka, who teamed up with us. As it turns out, he's a student at Harold Washington College! Talk about serendipity.

The campaign is going well. Senator McCain and the idiot woman Sarah Palin have proven themselves to be incompetent for the jobs, especially after McCain's silly remark that "the economy is strong," and even sillier stunt of suspending his campaign to focus on fixing the economic meltdown.

Even though the tide seems to be moving in the right direction for the Obama campaign, the reality is we're still in America where race seems to trump everything else. I pray things will turn out fine. Lord knows, I'm doing my part.

My prayer today is:

"Dear Heavenly Father,
Please continue to use me for the purposes that you see fit;
And bless me and Mom with good health, peace and love.
And if it is your will, please bless this country with an Obama victory tonight.
In Jesus' name, I pray.
Amen."

CHAPTER

Six

ELECTION DAY

THE GENERAL ELECTION – 2008
The Lead-Up to Election Day

All of us supporting the Democratic ticket of Obama/Biden were ecstatic and hope-filled after the DNC Convention. That euphoria was short-lived after the one-two punches from then-Alaska Governor Sarah Palin at the RNC Convention in Minnesota held the day after the close of the Democratic convention.

"You know the difference between a hockey mom and a pit bull? Lipstick,"[26] she sniped about her toughness as compared to a weak Obama.

"I guess – I guess a small-town mayor is sort of like a community organizer, except that you have actual responsibilities."[27]

And that's how the RNC Convention opened and continued. One quip, one dig, one shot after another about Obama's inexperience, incompetence, elitism, liberalism and overall inability to lead the country. One speaker after another, the denigration continued. Not much talk about what the Republicans would do, but plenty about what the Democrats couldn't. Whereas our convention and platform had been about hope, theirs was about nope; ours had been about "yes we can," theirs was about "oh, no you can't." The contrast in the two conventions was

---

[26] Excerpt from the transcript "Sarah Palin – Speech at the Republican National Convention," *New York Times*, September 3, 2008 – U.S./Elections [http://elections.nytimes.com /2008/president/conventions/videos/20080828_OBAMA_SPEECH.html#].

[27] Ibid.

as stark as the two political ideologies themselves: progressive versus regressive, embracing the challenges of a brave new frontier versus a yearning to return to the way things were. After a week-long display of nearly white-only, middle-aged, conservative, male-dominated audiences enthusiastically cheering and lusting over the Barbie-doll-turned-beauty-queen-turned-small-town-mayor Sarah Palin, nearly all of the wind was pulled from the sails of the Democratic Party's momentum, that just days prior had soared.

I watched the television screen with dismay, not only at what was being said and the reactions of the crowds at the convention, but I also felt dismay at the generosity of warmth that Americans across the country were blanketing onto the cold, chilling governor of Alaska.

"Oh, no she didn't!" I said to the TV.

"No, no they're not clapping," I thought.

"Oh, yes they are," I responded.

"Oh, s**t! Maybe we can't," I said softly, flicking off the television, watching the screen fade into blackness.

The Republican momentum continued for a couple more weeks, before the first chink in Ms. Palin's armor surfaced during the Charlie Gibson interview:

GIBSON: "What insight into Russian actions, particularly in the last couple of weeks, does the proximity of the state give you?"

PALIN: "They're our next door neighbors and you can actually see Russia from land here in Alaska, from an island in Alaska."[28]

Chink.

GIBSON: "Do you agree with the Bush doctrine?"

PALIN: "In what respect, Charlie?"

GIBSON: "The Bush – well, what do you – what do you interpret it to be?"

PALIN: "His world view."[29]

Chink. Chink.

[28] *ABC News* anchor, Charlie Gibson, interviewed Sarah Palin on Thursday, September 11, 2008 in Fairbanks, Alaska.

[29] *ABC News* anchor, Charlie Gibson, interviewed Sarah Palin on Thursday, September 11, 2008 in Fairbanks, Alaska.

And then came the Katie Couric interview:

COURIC: "But he [John McCain] has been in Congress for 26 years. He's been chairman of the powerful Commerce Committee. And he has almost always sided with less regulation, not more."

PALIN: "He's also known as the maverick though, taking shots from his own party, and certainly taking shots from the other party. Trying to get people to understand what he's been talking about – the need to reform government."

COURIC: "But can you give me any other concrete examples? Because I know you've said Barack Obama is a lot of talk and no action. Can you give me any other examples in his 26 years of John McCain truly taking a stand on this?"

PALIN: "I can give you examples of things that John McCain has done, that has shown his foresight, his pragmatism, and his leadership abilities. And that is what America needs today."

COURIC: "I'm just going to ask you one more time – not to belabor the point. Specific examples in his 26 years of pushing for more regulation."

PALIN: "I'll try to find you some and I'll bring them to you."[30]
Another chink.

COURIC: "And when it comes to establishing your worldview, I was curious, what newspapers and magazines did you regularly read before you were tapped for this to stay informed and to understand the world?"

PALIN: "I've read most of them, again with a great appreciation for the press, for the media."

COURIC: "What, specifically?"

PALIN: "Um, all of them, any of them that have been in front of me all these years."

COURIC: "Can you name a few?"

PALIN: "I have a vast variety of sources where we get our news, too. Alaska isn't a foreign country, where it's kind of suggested, 'Wow,

<hr>

[30] *CBS Evening News* anchor Katie Couric conducted a series of interviews with Sarah Palin that aired on September 24, 2008, September 25, 2008 and September 30, 2008.

how could you keep in touch with what the rest of Washington, D.C., may be thinking when you live up there in Alaska?' Believe me, Alaska is like a microcosm of America."[31]

Double chink.

And then there was Tina Fey's dead-on ridicule of Sarah Palin during a *Saturday Night Live* skit mocking Ms. Palin for being able to "see Russia from my house!"[32]

Final chink, before the armor crumbled into pieces like broken peanut brittle, revealing a shallow Sarah Palin underneath.

ELECTION DAY IN THE CALL CENTER

Finally, the day had come. A day the country had chased for over a year. And at this point, a day for which the whole world waited – no, watched and waited – to see who would be the next leader of the free world. Would it be John McCain or Barack Obama? I felt the heaviness of the moment, felt that we were on the cusp of electing the first black president of America. I'd been increasingly involved with the campaign since its beginning, and was anxious to see it through to the end. I'd barely slept the night before. Rising early, I prayed, showered and made a slow, easy walk from the Downtown Chicago Sheraton to the National Headquarters.

The weather was unseasonably warm for November in Chicago, with a morning temperature in the low sixties. The high was predicted to reach the mid-seventies, more than 30 degrees above normal. Good weather encouraged higher voter turnout. I smiled at the early morning sun and budding humidity skimming my face as I walked along Upper Wacker Drive. I was scheduled to pull an 8 to 5 shift in the Call Center. Staff and volunteers from across the nation wanted to work in the NHQ Call Center on that day. Not only was it one of the nerve centers

---

[31] *CBS Evening News* anchor Katie Couric conducted a series of interviews with Sarah Palin. This response was part of the interview that aired on September 30, 2008.

[32] Doing a parody of Sarah Palin on *Saturday Night Live,* comedic actress Tina Fey used this line in a sketch titled "A Nonpartisan Message from Governor Palin & Senator Hilary Clinton" that aired on September 13, 2008.

of the campaign, but it was geographically located adjacent to the "war room," with only a temporary wall and hollow door separating the two. People who hadn't ever worked the Call Center tried pulling rank and/ or strings to get in. Stephanie (the new Call Center manager) was having none of that. The powers that be gave her complete autonomy over the Call Center, and she stood steadfast against the pressure of local organizations from other offices, field organizers from out of state, and interns who were the children of Mr. or Mrs. So-and-So. It didn't matter. Her philosophy was that those who had worked the phones through the rough and tumble times had earned their rightful place to work the Call Center on this day. The other reason, and perhaps the main one, was she in truth needed people who had experience working the phones; who knew how to navigate the campaign's website and databases to find call scripts, policy positions, phone message forms, voting irregularities forms, and campaign contribution forms; people who knew the names and voices of both in-state and out-of-state dignitaries; how to handle their calls, and when and where to transfer them if necessary. In short, she needed the best people that the campaign had trained and utilized for over a year: people like me, Sarah, Joyce, Kathy, Susan, Janet, Clarinda, Don Baird, Rosalyn Jamison, Denise Snyder, and many, many others.

And so it was. I cleared security, rode the elevator to the nineteenth floor, was buzzed in through the glass doors and took my seat in the front row, third seat in from the left.

"Thank you for calling Obama/Biden for America! This is Michelle. How may I help you?"

"Is Obama winning?" the anxious caller asked.

"Well, the polls just opened up an hour ago here, Ma'am," I responded.

"Well, do you think he's gonna win?"

"I sure hope so."

"I hope so, too. I got 4 to 1 odds on this race," the caller responded.

"Where are you calling from?"

"Fishers, Indiana."

"I canvassed in Fishers!" I responded. "I think we might turn that state blue."

"I hope so. I got a lotta green riding on this."

"Well, thank you for calling, Ma'am," I said with a slight sigh before releasing the call.

Not all participants in the campaign were involved because of civic duty or because of a passion for politics. Some saw the race as, well, a race, a contest, a gambler's big chance, a dog-and-pony show to enjoy from the sidelines. Some saw it as a historical phenomenon; others as a fulfillment of some spiritual oracle; while others viewed it as their last (or first) chance to "throw the bums out" for good. The one common thread with all of these callers was that politics is about *people*, the root for the word politics itself (whether from the ancient Greek word *polis* meaning city-state or the Old French word *cite* meaning city or *citeain* meaning citizen).[33] And because people are emotional, politics in turn is about emotions. Whether it was the emotion of civic responsibility, altruism, or opportunism and gambling, people were moved. And we heard from them all, from every corner of the globe.

"Obama/Biden for America! This is Michelle. How may I help you?"

"Hey! We're calling from Moneygall!" the excited caller said from the other end of the phone.

"Where?" I queried.

"Moneygall. Moneygall, Ireland! Obama's great-great-great-grandfather was raised here. Moneygall. Moneygall, Ireland!" several voices in the background repeated.

"Oh! Well, hello, Sir. How may I help you?"

"Just callin' to say that we're pulling for Obama over here. Tell 'im to win. Win for Moneygall!"

"I will. Sounds like there's quite a crowd where you are."

"'Tis. We're at the local pub, and we're pulling for 'im!"

"Well, thank you, Sir. I'll get the word up to him," I said before hanging up and thinking that it was a bit early for pubs, clubs, or celebrating. I quickly released that thought before proceeding on to the next calls.

---

[33] As defined at www.dictionary.com, provided by Collins English Dictionary.

By noon the turnout reports were being broadcast across all of the major networks and local television stations. Turnout was exceptionally high, with many states reporting lines of voters queuing for blocks and blocks. Some polling places were running low on ballots, some sites didn't have enough workers and security in place to open on time, others were reporting machine irregularities, while others were experiencing old-fashioned voter suppression tactics – especially in the South.

"Obama/Biden for Amer..."

"Theys cheating down here!" the caller interrupted.

"Where, Ma'am? What are they doing?" I asked.

"I'm calling from Texarkana, Texas. They saying I ain't on the list. But I better be! I got my new voter card in my hand! Lying bastards! I know I'm on the list!"

"Okay, Ma'am. Let me get your name and the polling place where you are. We have attorneys on hand just for situations like this. Don't worry. We'll get this straightened out for you," I assured her.

"Thank ya, Sweetie. I ain't gonna let these old bastards get away with this!"

Just like I'd done on primary election nights, I keyed the caller's information into the online form that we had in place. We also had hard-copy voting irregularity forms to complete and hand-deliver to a group of volunteers, mostly lawyers, who were on duty that day to handle these types of situations. There were roughly fifty volunteers in this special "election day" unit, each one assigned to a state or region. They had listings of the names and cell numbers of local attorneys in each state who were part of the "voter protection" team. The "special unit" of volunteers took the voting complaint information given to them and phoned it in to the attorneys at or near polling places across the country. Within a short time span, the local attorneys could intervene and inquire about the voting irregularities. The whole process was documented, with the original forms being handed off to representatives, also lawyers, from the Democratic National Committee, who would in turn later investigate and bring charges as warranted.

Although the atmosphere in the "special unit" was tense and noisy, somehow the layers of watchdogging ran as smoothly as a relay race team, with each of us passing the baton to the next to finish the race. Knowing that a system was in place to protect their vote also seemed to ease voters' anxiety.

"Obama/Biden for America! This is Michelle. How may I help you?"

"Great! I got Michelle!"

"Yes, this is Michelle. How may I help you?"

"I'm calling from a local news station in Missouri, and I'd like to interview you, Mrs. Obama."

"Oh, no, I'm not Mrs. Obama. I'm another Michelle."

"How long have you two been married?"

"Sir, I'm not Mrs. Obama. Do you really think she'd be answering the phones on Election Day?" I rebuffed.

"Well, I know she works the campaign and sometimes answers the phones. So, what has it been like going through the campaign? How has it been for your kids?"

"Sir, for the last time, I'm not Mrs. Obama. Can I help you with something else!" I said excitedly.

"Yes, just tell me your anniversary date?"

"Okay, Sir, I'm going to end the call now."

"Okay, Mrs. Obama. It was good talking to you."

With a roll of my eyes, I hung up the telephone. Stephanie and I locked eyes. Then Noah and I locked eyes. Then Kathy and Sarah and I locked eyes. They'd all heard my end of the conversation and knew what was going on, and in a blink we all burst into a fit of laughter. It was the first time that day that I'd gotten the "Michelle question." The ironic part is that another Michelle, a young white woman, also worked the same shift as me and never got the question. With my blended Dixie-Midwestern accent and Southern drawl, my voice has its own distinct uniqueness. For sure, nothing like the perfectly pitched Michelle Obama, yet none of us could explain why I consistently got that question or what it was that callers on the other end really heard or believed in their mind's ear. We laughed at the ridiculousness and repeated persistence of this marvel. It also provided some levity and a perfect pause to forge a break.

Downstairs, sitting underneath an umbrella-covered table outside, I finished my coffee and dialed up James.

"Hi, Sweetie!"

"Hey," James replied.

"How's it going out there?"

"Good."

"Picked up anybody yet?"

"Well, no," he said a bit disappointedly. "I'm actually canvassing. That's where they said they need me most."

"Oh?"

"It's cool. I talked to Cathe. Bruce is driving people to the polls in Dove Creek."

"Really?"

"Yeah."

"Cool," I responded.

"Yeah. Well, I'm about to ring a doorbell. I better go," he said.

"Okay, Sweetie."

"See you tonight."

"Yeah, in Grant Park," I replied.

"Cool."

"Cool," I repeated.

James was in Gary, Indiana trying to help turn that state blue. He'd been assigned to driving people to the polls but was needed to do door-to-door canvassing instead. He'd worked the streets of Gary a couple of months back when he and I and my coworker Dr. Don Baird along with Francis Motycka, a Harold Washington College student, had canvassed together. Gary was an overwhelmingly Democratic city, but its turnout numbers were historically low. We'd been told as low as 15%. James's job, along with others out there that day, was to make sure that registered voters actually voted. While he worked Gary, Indiana, his sister and brother-in-law worked the rural towns of Colorado. We were all part of the 50-state volunteer force trying to turn purple and red states blue. I smiled inside and out at the thought of all of us: me; James; Denise and

Mike; our friend Rosalyn Jamison and her friends in the south suburbs of Chicago; my sister and brother-in-law, Debra and Dean Muhammad, in Atlanta; her sons Alfonso Daniel and Edward Clay; their girlfriends Tanesha and Traci; James's sister and brother-in-law, Catherine and Bruce Hill, in Dove Creek, Colorado; and our friend Dr. Cynthia Barnes in Denver; all of us linked together like a giant fence encircling America and pushing her citizenry to get out and vote.

I sat for a few moments more and reminisced about my first days in the Call Center; about the first time I'd been mistaken for Michelle Obama; about how completely serendipitous it was that our mothers had named us both Michelle and how this invisible fence of hope had brought us two Michelles together. Today would be my last day working the campaign, and I wanted to do all that I could to help get us across the finish line. I soaked up the last few minutes of cool air and warm sunshine before returning to the Call Center and to being "the other Michelle" for one last time.

ELECTION NIGHT

I'd finished my shift at the Call Center, leaving behind the buzzing atmosphere of ringing phones, excited callers, nervous volunteers and on-edge staffers. Today would be the last day that many of us would see each other. After much picture-taking, hugging, handshakes, back pats, and number exchanging, I made my way over to Stephanie's, Sarah's and Noah's desks.

"Well, this is it, huh?" I asked Noah.

"Yep," he replied in his usual Midwestern, to-the-point way.

"It was good working with ya," I replied.

He spread his arms for a big hug and said,

"Good working with you, too, Michelle. You kept the Call Center lively."

I moved over to Sarah's desk and hugged her, too, before working my over to Stephanie.

"I'll miss you guys," I said, a bit choked up.

"I'll miss you, too. I really mean it," Stephanie replied.

I turned to leave and she called me back.

"Hey. I'm headed for D.C.," she said just above a whisper.

"Seriously?"

"Yeah! Pretty cool."

"Indeed! You deserve it, Stephanie. You really do," I replied.

"Thanks. Here, take this and enjoy yourself tonight," she said with a smile, as she pressed an Election Night ticket to the rally in Grant Park in my hand.

I smiled. She winked and I safely tucked the ticket into the side pocket of my purse, next to the one that the campaign had given to a select few volunteers.

James and I walked south on North Michigan Avenue. The streets of Chicago had been blocked off and traffic diverted for nearly five miles in each direction of Grant Park. Walking was the only way to get there. Even Lake Michigan, to the east of the park, was being guarded by security copters and boats. Crowds began forming in the early afternoon. Clumps of friends, families, students, out-of-towners and locals walked from the north, south and west points of the city. As predicted, the temperature hovered near the mid-seventies. Early dusk was approaching as the sun positioned itself for sleep. The soft rays of the early evening sun felt warm and assuring on our faces and backs and between the shoulder blades, as we strolled hand in hand. We had a mile's walk between us and the rally site. We walked in silence, not needing to talk to communicate. We knew what the other was thinking: *We did it. This is it. We've seen this fight through to the finish. Now, let's go stand among the other grassroots soldiers and claim our victory.* Or something like that.

The Illinois polls would be closing in just a few minutes. We picked up our pace for a couple of blocks, and suddenly without words, stopped. We looked at each other with raised brows that said "Are you thinking what I'm thinking?" I responded, "Yes." We turned and headed back north, towards the Downtown Hyatt. Being part of the fifty-plus club, having worked the campaign all day, a bit hot, a bit tired, standing in a crowd of tens of thousands was a bit much.

The Hyatt was the official hotel for the Obama victory party. People had started gathering in the big, open bar of the hotel located on the mezzanine level. We joined the swelling crowd and scouted about for seats. A gentleman at the bar yielded his seat for me, and James stood nearby. The place was loud with murmurs and chuckles and head-back laughter. We ordered ice-cold beers and deli sandwiches. Suspended from nearly every corner of the ceiling were 52-inch television screens set on CNN and MSNBC. The polls were closed in Illinois and across the Midwest. Wolf Blitzer of CNN stood before a huge map of the United States, whereby each state would illuminate blue or red, respectively, depending on whether Obama (the Democrat) or McCain (the Republican) won that state. Two states had been called: Vermont for Obama, Kentucky for McCain. The middle of the map illuminated blue. Obama had just won Illinois. The crowd roared! MSNBC lagged by a few seconds in calling the winner and changing its map's color. Illinois turned blue on MSNBC. The crowd roared, again.

The atmosphere was festive and light. Strangers were huddled close and drinking, sharing barstools and campaign stories. A pleasant, white couple from Louisville, Kentucky, sat to our left, and a group of fun-loving black college kids gathered to our right. We all talked, laughed, shared stories, swapped emails and business cards. The maps quickly bled blue along the New England coast and northeast corridor as Obama won Connecticut, D.C., Maine, Massachusetts, New Hampshire and New Jersey.[34] The bar crowd went crazy with yelling. The atmosphere was electric with jubilance and frantic excitement. People literally sat on the edges of their seats, watching the maps as if tuned into the latest blockbuster thriller. The anticipation of an Obama victory was building. My heart was racing, and so was James's. He stood close behind me. I could feel its thump-thump-thumping rhythm as I leaned against his torso, which served as a backrest to my barstool. Another state on the map turned blue. Obama had won the hard-fought Pennsylvania!

"Yeah-h-h!" the crowd screamed. "YES WE CAN! YES WE CAN!"

Two more states turned colors – red. McCain had taken Arkansas and Alabama. We'd been there for over an hour, drinking steadily and

---

[34] Election night returns by state available at CNN's *Election Center* 2008, http://www.cnn.com/ELECTION/2008/ results/president/.

celebrating. And even in my elated and hazy state, I noticed a curious pattern to the states that the two candidates were winning. State by state, from West Virginia to Kentucky to Tennessee through Arkansas, all along the backbone of the Appalachians, the map bled red. The small-town hominess and Christian conservatism of Sarah Palin had won the hearts and votes of hardscrabble coal workers and poor whites in the South. At the same time, the middle of the country above the Mason-Dixon Line was blossoming deep blue; in places where generations of blacks had migrated from the misery of the South and where liberal whites had supported the civil rights movement, the women's movement, and fought against the Viet Nam war with blood, sweat and tears. I looked at the map and had to silently admit that we live in two Americas: one moving progressively towards the future, leaving a trail of blue dust behind; the other moving back to the good ol' days of the glorious South, leaving a bloodstained trail of red in its tracks. The electoral count was 82 for Obama, 39 for McCain – 188 more electoral votes to go before Obama would reach the winning total. The night was young, the crowd happy. The drinks were flowing and clock ticking. The counts were trickling in and adding up in Obama's favor.

New York went for Obama.

The crowd roared. That meant 31 more electoral votes, 157 more to go.

Michigan, Minnesota, Rhode Island and Wisconsin spread more blue across the middle of America – 95 more votes to go.

"YES WE CAN! YES WE CAN!"

The TV pundits began discussing the purple states that were traditionally red but were leaning blue for this election; where the polls had closed, but were too close to call: North Carolina, Virginia and Colorado. More results came in: Ohio, Iowa, New Mexico, all for Obama.

"Yeah, baby!"

Obama had 207 electoral votes, 63 to go.

The air was thick with anticipation and the smell of booze and beer. Keith Olbermann and Chris Matthews were talking on MSNBC. Would Colorado and Nevada go from red to purple to blue? They bantered.

Even if they didn't, the former red states of Florida and Virginia, with their collective 40 votes, were still too close to call. Obama needed only 63 more electoral votes. The polls on the West Coast were closing, and California sat out there with 55 big, fat votes lying in waiting, almost guaranteed to be blue. The math was easy. Obama was on a path to victory.

"YES WE CAN!" the crowd chanted.

And at 10 p.m. local time, almighty California rolled in with its huge 55 votes for Obama! The West Coast tidal wave continued: Oregon, Washington and Hawaii all called for Obama, making his electoral vote count 284.[35]

"YES WE CAN! YES WE CAN!"

The bar crowd jumped up and cheered, chanting and yelling as stranger upon stranger hugged and kissed cheeks, becoming family in the process. Many of us were too young to have marched in the civil rights protests, too young to have served in Viet Nam. This was our cause, our movement, our fight, and we'd won. We were happy. We were proud. We'd come together and done something no other generations of Americans had done – we'd voted in the first African American president of the United States.

I basked in the glory of that moment. As the pundits smiled and talked fast, and the crowd in Grant Park celebrated, I stood still and basked in the moment, thinking about the long haul from the small group home conference calls in Georgia to the snowy trails of Iowa; from the miles-long, sweaty walk in Denver to canvassing the battered streets of Gary, Indiana; from the thousands upon thousands of calls taken in the Call Center to the victory tonight; and now it was over. It took me a few moments to wrap this reality around my reminiscences. I felt a mixture of joy, pride, sadness, and longing for more. But it was over. The campaign had ended, and the team I'd spent a year and half with were transitioning to the presidency. I was going to miss them, miss that part of my life.

I grabbed James's hand, the hand of the man who had been by my

---

[35] Election night returns by state available at CNN's *Election Center* 2008, http://www.cnn.com/ELECTION/2008/ results/president/.

side during this exciting and tiring journey. We locked arms and walked out into the crowds that had formed on the streets of Chicago. The whole city celebrated. One of our own had just been elected president and leader of the free world. The whole city was electric with celebration. We passed a young man along our walk. He wore an Obama tee-shirt and broad grin.

"Yes we can!" he yelled.

No, son, I thought. *Yes we did.*

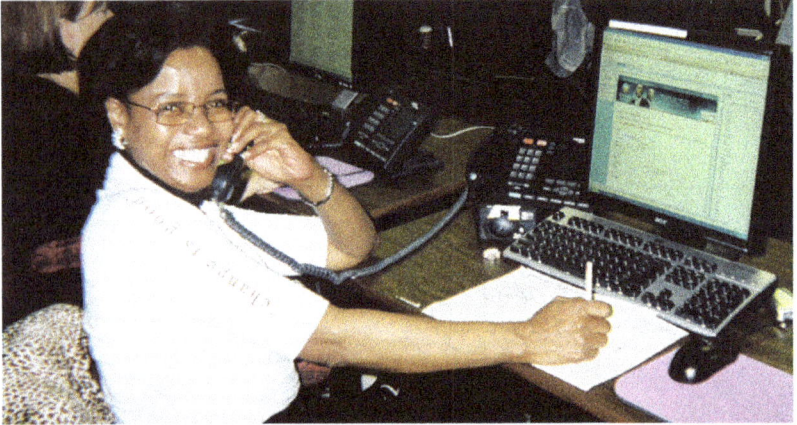

2008 Election Night at the National Headquarters in Chicago. Me working the phones and posing with Call Center managers Stephanie and Noah.

James, me, Rosalyn, Denise, Mike and Dr. Donald Baird canvassing in Gary,
Indiana on Dr. Baird's birthday – October 25, 2008.

Me, Rosalyn and Denise volunteering at a rally in Highland, Indiana on Halloween 2008.

Candidate Obama addressing the crowd.

CHAPTER

Seven

WASHINGTON, D.C. & THE PTT

This part of the telling of my experience is a challenge in that I must tread carefully between not revealing too much, which would violate the "Obama-Biden Transition Project Code of Ethical Conduct" agreement that I signed, and revealing so little as to not be of any interest or educational value to the reader. The goals of sharing this part of my story are to provide insight into what goes on in a presidential transition office in general; to explain some of the operational goings-on of the Obama-Biden Transition Project in particular; and to provide a bottom-up, behind-the-scenes look into an experience that I think most of us have neither had nor perhaps even thought about having.

I must say upfront that I don't have juicy or salacious stories to share. Neither I nor any of the other volunteer staff were part of high-level, closed-door meetings. I didn't make decisions that shook the earth or moved the transition team in any form or manner. During this time, I wasn't even in the same room with President-Elect Obama, Vice President-Elect Joseph Biden, Rahm Emmanuel, David Axelrod, Valerie Jarrett, or most of any other senior staff. I was, however, an element in the lubricant that kept the wheel moving. Just as I had been many months prior during the campaign, I was once again going to be one of the voices from a call center that represented now President-Elect Obama, answering questions and connecting people with the information that they needed. And while that may not sound like much of a role, just know that of the more than seven hundred volunteers who had worked in the NHQ Call Center in Chicago, I was one of four who was called to serve with the transition team. In part, I believe it was because Stephanie needed trained people who could walk through the doors knowing exactly what to do and how to handle the calls. Other reasons, I think, included the possibility that many people could not have gotten away from their jobs and lives for the eight weeks required; and in part because, to a lesser degree, not everyone who'd volunteered in the campaign had a ready-to-roll professional wardrobe of suits and attire that would blend in with the D.C. crowd of policy wonks and politicians; and in part because of my mellow yet pleasant personality that seems to put most people at ease; but mostly, because I was someone whom Stephanie liked and trusted. And it is that trust that I intend to honor as I carefully, yet as fully as I can, talk about my experience on the Obama-Biden Transition Project, aka the Presidential Transition Team (PTT). With that said, here's how this part of my story unfolds.

THE CALL TO SERVE

You should come out here and work for the Transition Team. I really need good people who can help me in the Call Center here. What do you say? Let me know.
– Stephanie

I stared at the email in absolute disbelief. For twenty-two months the Obama Presidential Campaign had been a huge part of my life. Just saying "good-bye," "so long," "nice working with you," to my former campaign-mates didn't feel right, or offer closure; and settling into the routine of work/home/work/home/going out occasionally with friends was a more difficult transition than I'd imagined.

And so, here I sat, staring blurry eyed at an email message from Stephanie Fine (former NHQ Call Center Manager, now PTT Call Center Manager) asking me to join her in D.C. A hundred different questions whirled through my mind:

Is this for real?
What would I be doing?
What could I do that no else could?
Why me?
Why not me?

What does Volunteer Staff mean?
Will I get paid?
Will I get room and board in lieu of money?
If not, can I afford to go?
Can I afford not to go?
Would I be crazy to turn down such an opportunity?
Where will I stay?
Can I get off work for eight weeks?
If not, then what?
If so, then what?

The more questions I answered, the more were raised. I studied the email for a while longer and answered Stephanie with a great big thanks and a request to get back to her in a couple of days after talking to my supervisor and family.

"Mommie! Guess what?" I shouted at my mother after racing upstairs to her bedroom.

"What?" she replied, quite startled.

"I've been asked to work on the Obama Presidential Transition Team!"

"Oh my God! Really? In D.C.?"

"Yeah, can you believe it?"

"No, um, yes. When do you leave? How long will you be gone? How much are you getting paid?"

All reasonable questions, though none of which I had answers to.

"I don't know," was the most honest and the best I could muster.

I wasn't sure of what to do, but knew exactly who to ask for help.

"Hi, Sweetie!"

"Hey," James responded.

"You'll never guess what happened to me today!"

A rather long, excited explanation of my day ensued before I asked him if he thought I should go.

"Well, Michelle. The way I see it, Barack Obama has asked you to come to D.C. to help him with his transition to the White House. Do you really want to tell the next president of the United States no?"

"No, of course not. But Obama didn't ask me. Stephanie did."

"Oh, I'm sorry. Doesn't Stephanie work for Obama?"

"Yes," I replied.

"Don't the people who are working for him represent him?"

"Yes."

"Then like I asked before, do you really want to say no to President-Elect Obama?"

He'd done it again, pressed logic against my emotional fog and punched a gaping hole straight through it. Two weeks later, on November 28, 2008, I was heavily packed and standing in line ready to board Amtrak's train number 35 – *The Capitol Limited*. This journey was taking me away from my family and friends and James for nearly two months. I was nervous and scared, but kept moving forward. I understood the sadness in my mother's eyes – not the kind of sadness that drenches over you at the news of a death, but a sadness rooted in missing that person's company, rooted in a sense of worry and concern, a sadness that is innate in a mother saying good-bye to her baby girl. I understood that sadness, because I felt it too.

I was going to miss my mother, and Denise, and Mickey and Cheryl, and Diretha, and going to my church on Sunday mornings, and most of all, I was going to miss James. I was missing him already. Yes, I understood the apprehension that my mother was experiencing. It was all knotted up inside of me as well, along with feelings of joy, pride, privilege and adventure.

The waiting room smelled of people a bit overdressed for the mild winter weather and who were perhaps beginning to sweat; of noisy babies in need of dry diapers; and of hotdogs and nachos that people ate, using their laps as table tops. It was crowded – warm and crowded. It was the Thanksgiving holiday season after all. Crowds were to be expected. I shuffled along in line behind about a dozen Amish people; behind a white couple escorting their son back to college; behind a young brother in flip-flops looking curiously at a shapely young woman behind me who had prominent black features, light freckled skin, and long, beautiful red hair.

I slowly moved through the boarding entrance, pausing long enough to absorb the sights, smells and sounds of the train station, searing in my memory one last look at my beloved Chicago, a place that I wouldn't see for the next eight weeks.

❦

THE FIRST MONTH ~
DECEMBER 2008

It was time. I was roughly four blocks from the fictitious address they'd given us. Because the office location for the Presidential Transition Team (PTT) was a secret, we were given a made-up address between two actual cross streets on Sixth Street. I was only two blocks away, so I slowly made my way over to Sixth Street, left turn off of D Street and halfway to getting to E Street was this audacious red brick building with a series of glass doors marked either "Enter Only" or "Do Not Enter." And, like something out of a Harry Potter book, I spotted the address "451 Sixth" stenciled on a white poster board on an easel propped near the entrance doors. *Clever,* I thought. The sign was inconspicuous enough that if you weren't looking for the make-believe address, you wouldn't have ever noticed it or known what it meant if you did notice. Those who knew, knew. All others could only guess or just pass right by it. I knew, so I turned in and entered the building.

"Your name's not on the list!" an officer at the security window shouted through the thick glass, shoving my passport back through the slot in the window.

"Excuse me?" I questioned in wide-eyed disbelief.

He repeated what he'd said before, except slower and even louder as if talking to a foreigner or lip-reader. "Call your contact and let 'em know that you're not on the list."

I grabbed my passport, rumpled email letter, and low-battery cell phone and walked over to the row of seats that the officer had pointed towards. I attempted to call Melissa, but my phone was completely dead.

"Damn!"

Within twenty minutes the computer glitch between the PTT's and Secret Service's systems was fixed, and suddenly I was on the list.

"Michelle Carnes!"

"Yes Sir, that's me!" I responded as I hurriedly gathered my things and moved across the room to the security window.

"Your badge, Ma'am," the officer said, sliding my PTT badge through the window slot. "Punch in the numbers on the back to get through the security gate."

"Yes Sir!"

I looked down at the blue badge he'd handed me. My stadium picture from Denver smiled back at me. Beneath the picture was my name and beneath that was the title, "Staff," and beneath that in bold, capital letters was the acronym PTT. And finally, on each side of the picture on the badge was a column of hologram stars with "Office of the Secret Service" embossed at the center.

Wow! was all I could think. *I'm here, really here, on the inside and, albeit small, a part of President-Elect Obama's transition team.*

THE PHYSICAL LAYOUT OF THE PTT

The new staff orientation started at 3 p.m. Melissa led the way, as a cluster of twenty or so of us gathered around her, listening and looking. It was an impressive place. The PTT took up three floors of the Judiciary Building. (I can now reveal the real location of the PTT, since it became public information within a month of our being there. At the time, however, keeping our location secret was a high priority.) Lawyers, judges and other judiciary workers had been temporarily displaced to accommodate us. Cherry, mahogany and other dark woods framed the opaque walls and doorways, and worked quite well against the contrasting sky-blue carpeting that ran throughout the offices, meeting rooms and long hallways. The conference rooms, encased with the kind of thick, rippling glass usually seen on shower doors at a kitchen and bath expo, were large with long, dark tables and leather swivel chairs. Melissa guided us up a few floors where a veranda with a panoramic view of downtown D.C. sat off from one of the large corner offices. It was beautiful being able to see the dome-shaped rooftops of all of the important buildings of the nation's capital. We wound our way down through the building, with Melissa pointing out key areas along the way: the waiting area for visitors on the main floor; the Press Room in the basement; the mailroom; the fall-out shelter. We ended the tour in the Press Room, where the orientation was to be held. We'd needed that tour and relaxing views to get us loosened up for what was coming next.

The orientation included a series of presentations from representatives of various governmental departments, mainly from the GSA – General Services Administration. The first presenter talked about operational, procedural matters like whom to call if there were computer problems, how to get office supplies, what do if your badge wasn't letting you through the security gate. Useful, but pretty benign stuff. The next presenter discussed personnel issues, i.e., how to complete insurance forms, travel forms, or request sick leave. Next up was a young man who discussed a lot of procedural stuff too, except he talked about the kinds of stuff that could kill you: what to do in the event of a bomb threat; how to evacuate and where to go; what happened to mail and packages that were sent to President-Elect Obama, or to anyone in his immediate family, or to anyone on his transition team; and what happened when something poisonous or deadly was contained inside. Included below is a partial recounting of that discussion:

1. For security purposes, all mail addressed to President-Elect Obama and his family, including his mother-in-law; to Vice President-Elect Biden; and other high-ranking officials on the transition team was intercepted and routed to an off-site facility. At this location, mail and packages underwent a 12-point security check, which included x-rays, ultraviolet and radioactive tests, sniff tests, and hand searches.

2. The types of Items that were discarded included the following:
   a. Junk Mail: advertisements such as postcards, leaflets, pamphlets, fliers, circulars, catalogs and any other non-solicited offers
   b. Periodicals (newspapers and magazines)
   c. Food Items: perishable items such as fruit, candy, cakes, meats, cheese, tea, flowers, etc.

    d.   Liquid Items: such as wine bottles, perfumes, house-
hold cleaners, etc.

    e.   Sharp Items: such as syringe needles, razors, nails, or
other items with sharp edges

    f.   Animal or Animal Parts: such as taxidermy items, ani-
mal skins, furs, leathers, scales, stuffed bodies, etc.

    g.   Non-Living/Living Organic Materials: such as stones,
rocks, leaves, tree branches, plants, etc.

3.   Items such as letters, drawings, books, etc., that did make it
through the mail screening process were stamped with a date
and inspector's number, then forwarded on to the PTT mailroom for distribution.

Up next was a young, chiseled, small-framed woman named Kelly
from the Office of the Secret Service. She stood wide-legged, ticking off
her fingers with each command she issued to us.

"NUMBER ONE: tell NO ONE that you work for the PTT! Got
it?"

"Yes," we murmured back.

"NUMBER TWO: give NO ONE, including your closest friends
and family, the address of the PTT! Okay?"

"Okay," we recited like scared school children.

"Take off your badges before going outside. And IMMEDIATELY
report it if it's lost or stolen! Understand?"

"Yes Ma'am."

"And for God sakes, especially to you ladies, don't get loose at the
lips while playing around at one of these D. C. bars. Believe me, there
are reporters out there, snoops, and terrorists. Once they get wind that
you're part of the PTT, you'll become a target. For people who are des-
perate to get next to Obama, you are the closest tool they have to use.
And yes ladies, guys will SAY ANYTHING, and will DO ANYTHING
to get you to talk. SO DON'T!"

Kelly finished by asking if any of us had questions. I panned the
faces of the group sitting near me. No hands went up. The only ques-

tion on my mind after such a fear-evoking presentation was, *May I be excused now to go smoke a cigarette?*

We were escorted back upstairs to the Call Center, where we all were scheduled to work. Stephanie was giving the orientation. She greeted me with a broad smile and open arms.

"Michelle!" she said, giving me a close, tight, familiar hug.

"Hey, Stephanie!" I shouted. "It's so good to see you!"

This was the first we'd seen each other since Election Day, and it felt good. She was the one who'd asked me to come to D.C., to help her and Noah in the Call Center. We were both happy that I'd made it. We held each other for a moment longer before composing ourselves. She turned to the rest of the group and introduced herself, then began the orientation of Call Center operations. She explained the new phone system, the call scripts and the dos and don'ts of handling calls. I partly listened, but mostly observed and soaked in the feel of the place where I'd be working for the next couple of months.

It was small, quiet, almost austere and yet impressive. There were actual cubicles instead of the rows and rows of telephones like we had at the NHQ in Chicago. Each cubicle was equipped with wide-screen computer monitors, swivel chairs, bottled water and a phone system with the ability to "aux" or be removed from the queue if one needed to step away from the phones. There were about a dozen phone stations with room for another half-dozen workspaces for non-telephone work. The Call Center was situated between a massive coatroom to the left, with space enough to store all of our winter outer garments, boots, bags and personal computers; and to the right was a Starbucks-styled WiFi lounge. Restrooms, full-service break rooms and photocopy rooms occupied each end of the long, carpeted corridors. Every conceivable workplace comfort was in place to take the edge off of the long, tense workdays that awaited us. This setup was very different from the one in Chicago. We were no longer part of a campaign, but transitioning to an administration. The setting was more polished and professional, kicked up a few notches. Just the feel of the place told me that we were a part of something big and important. Like Dorothy in the movie *The Wizard of Oz*, all I could think was, *Toto, I've a feeling we're not in Kansas anymore.*

PTT OPERATIONS

As with past presidential transition teams, the Obama-Biden Transition Project's primary purposes were: (a) to hire key personnel to work in the White House and administration; and (b) to fine-tune the key policies on which the administration would focus.[36] Where this transition team differed, I was told by more than one person who had worked for the Clinton-Gore Transition Team, was in how inclusive, open, transparent and connected to voters it remained. Hence, the need for a PTT Call Center that would act as the voice of the transition team; would impart needed information and assistance to callers; would patiently hear out voter comments, complaints and inquiries; and would be that front-line conduit between the voter and the budding administration. To these ends, all PTT volunteers, irrespective of specialized skills, number of degrees, pedigree or political connection, started out on equal footing. We all started in the Call Center. This was the testing ground to sort those who were serious about being of service to the transition team from those who were simply auditioning for an administration job; those who could take orders well from those who could not; and those who could handle calls from the simple "yes or no" variety, to the complex, weird, personal and delicate, to the diplomatic and international, from those who felt that type of work was beneath them or was just simply too taxing. And during my eight-week tenure at the PTT, I saw a few people come and quietly go. They were the ones who couldn't take directions, or weren't getting hired on fast enough or got a better offer elsewhere. For the vast majority of us, we stayed and worked and, although we were at the bottom of the organizational totem poll, answered the calls with pride.

A few days after the election, and well before I arrived on December 1st, the highly efficient IT department had up and running a new website for the transition period: http://change.gov. The site was chock full

---

[36] The Scope of the purpose and responsibilities of the Presidential Transition Team as defined at http://change.gov/learn/transition.

of information on what the transition team was; who the major players were; how to apply for a job; where to call if you had a problem applying; how to comment and/or submit policy ideas to the transition team. All of which brought voters in contact with those of us manning the phones in the Call Center. With the help of the website, call scripts and organizational charts that we'd been given during orientation, I quickly began to understand the organizational structure of the transition team:

- At the very top were President-Elect Obama, Vice President-Elect Biden and the Obama-Biden Transition Project Co-Chairs John Podesta, Valerie Jarrett and Peter Rouse. David Axelrod, Rahm Emanuel and Robert Gibbs, all with designations of "special advisors," were outside of the structure and for a while worked closely with Obama in Chicago before joining the team in Washington, D.C.

- The next stratum down was a myriad of former government agency professionals that comprised the "The Advisory Board." Some of the members included William Daley, former Secretary of Commerce; Janet Napolitano, Governor of Arizona (at the time); and Susan Rice, former Assistant Secretary of State.[37]

- Next came senior staff members of the PTT, which included Stephanie Cutter, Chief Spokesperson; Cassandra Butts, General Counsel; Melody Barnes, Co-Director of Agency Review; and Michael Strautmanis, Director of Public Liaison and Intergovernmental Affairs.

- The next link in the chain was the Agency Review Teams. *"The Agency Review Teams for the Obama-Biden Transition will complete a thorough review of key departments, agencies and commissions of the United States government, as well as the White House, to provide the President-elect, Vice President-elect, and key advisors with information needed to make strategic policy, budgetary, and personnel decisions prior to the inauguration. The Teams will ensure that senior appointees have the information necessary to complete the confirmation process, lead their departments,*

---

[37] Listing of members of the advisory board provided at http://change.gov/learn/transition staff.

and begin implementing signature policy initiatives immediately after they are sworn in."[38] These were the people for whom we eventually directly worked.

- At the bottom of the chart was us – the corps of nearly 400 volunteers working four-, six- and seven-hour shifts, six days a week, answering calls and gradually taking on other duties of support.

THE WORK ITSELF

The volunteer staff comprised mostly professional people who'd put in a lot of time working the campaign. Some of us were people on leave from government or political professions; or educators and academics on winter break; business entrepreneurs with flexible work schedules; and attorneys, law clerks and law students of all stripes. We'd come from across the country, but mainly from the D.C. area and the Mid-Atlantic region. Our role was to provide support to the transition in whatever manner of help that was needed, which fell into four primary areas of duties: (1) answering calls in the Call Center; (2) conducting research for Agency Review Teams (or ARTs, as we called them); (3) copying, scanning, and emailing the myriad of letters, documents, agendas and meeting minutes that were later uploaded online for the "legacy files"; and (4) if selected, to work exclusively as an assistant to one of the team leaders of an ART.

All volunteer staff had to work an obligatory three-week stint in the Call Center. Calls fell into two main categories: typical inquiries about applying for jobs and job application status; and "activist calls," whereby an organization had strongly urged its membership to conduct a call-in campaign against a particular issue. As word got out that the transition had a toll-free telephone line, the call volume increased each day. By the end of my first week, based on in-house statistics, over 100,000 people had applied for positions. By the end of my first month, over 300,000 people had applied for jobs, many of whom were calling in.

[38] Definition and descriptions of agency review teams at http://change.gov/learn/obama_biden_transition_agency_review_teams.

Activists calls were pretty easy to identify. Callers used the exact same words, or actually read their scripts, or oftentimes outright told us that so-and-so organization asked them to call. The first of these calls that I remember was a call-in campaign to encourage Obama to forcefully speak out against the recent violence in Gaza where Israel had bombed and killed more than 225 and wounded over 600 Palestinians, in retaliation against Hamas in Palestine for, a few days prior, shooting rocket and mortar fire that killed four Israelis.[39] Not only did we receive hundreds of calls from Palestinian, Israeli and other groups that were against Israel's actions, but by five o'clock that evening a protest group of roughly 200 people were picketing outside of the PTT building. As with all calls, we'd type out the comments of the caller, mark the category or type of call and email the log to Stephanie or Noah. The calls regarding the Israeli-Palestinian conflict lasted for a day and a half. On another occasion, one of the funniest of the activist calls came when Obama proposed paying for State Children Health Insurance Programs (SCHIP) by increasing the federal tobacco tax. Mainly people from the "tobacco states" of the Carolinas, Kentucky and Tennessee called in to protest the tax increase, but they had no real argument for opposing funding child health care other than a higher cigarette tax would force them to quit smoking. Many of them were unfamiliar with the whole issue of the proposed tax increase and thus were unfamiliar with what the acronym SCHIP stood for, frequently calling it "S-SHIP," or "C-CHIP," or just plain old "that CHIP program." One man stuttered so badly as he read his script, I ended up finishing it for him. He finally admitted that he'd gotten the quote from a handout given to him at the cigarette depot along with a request to give the transition office a call. I felt bad for the guy. Being a smoker too, and not wanting to pay more for my cigarettes either, I still couldn't justify standing in the way of children getting access to health care and hopefully never becoming smokers themselves.

Other activist calls included protests against the appointment of re-

---

[39] Full NYT story entitled "Israeli Attack Kills Scores Across Gaza," available at http://www.nytimes.com/2008/12/27/world/africa/27iht-28mideast.18950014.html.

tired admiral Dennis Blair as Director of National Intelligence. Many people spoke passionately about his alleged role in torture and other violations of human rights. Some of them were veterans or spouses and families of veterans. Other callers were from various liberal groups who read from their scripts and often referred to Dennis Blair as "Tony Blair," former Prime Minister of Britain, instead. We logged the calls, counted the number of calls, and provided the statistics up the chain of command. In the end, Obama appointed Dennis Blair as Director of National Intelligence anyway. Of all of the activist calls, none were more vocal, vigilant or vile than the protest calls against Pastor Rick Warren of Saddleback Church giving the invocation at the Presidential Inauguration swearing-in ceremony. Progressive groups from the left side of the political spectrum that supported gay rights, women's rights, and pro-choice called in. Conservative groups from the right side of the political spectrum protested an "abortion rights-supporting Obama" selecting an evangelical minister in the first place. These callers did not use scripts. They spoke straight from the heart and gut. One that I recall vividly was a conversation with a gay man from Los Angeles:

"Good morning. Thank you for calling the Obama-Biden Presidential Transition. This is Michelle. How may I help you?"

"You can help me by letting that skinny little bastard Obama know that there's one gay man in California who is sorry that he voted for 'em! And if he lets that Rick Warren character give the invocation, he is a one-term president!"

"Well sir, he isn't in office yet. So, let's give him a chance to get in before we vote him out."

"My ass! Obama betrayed us! A lot of gay people voted for him. Just like black people, *WE* have been discriminated against, *OUR* human rights violated. Hell, we can't even get married! You hear what I'm saying?"

"Yes sir, I'm listening. I'm a black person, so I certainly understand discrimination, racism and any other 'ism', but I'm not ready to get rid of Obama before he can even take office."

"Yeah, well maybe because you're a gay-bashing, homophobe, too. B_*_H!"

Click.

Calls like that went on for over a week. They were relentless, totaling in the thousands. It was tiring. I was growing weary of them. We all were. In the end, Obama stuck by his choice of Rick Warren, and the protest calls stopped.

When volunteer staffers weren't working the phones, we were assisting with research for an Agency Review Team that needed information "yesterday." The work pace at the PTT was frantic. Not with people running around, or shouting, or scurrying about, but with people always either face down writing or checking off lists, or face up staring at the computer monitor and typing. The frantic part came in the form of all the various departments needing the research *now*; or for a meeting a few hours from now; or for a presentation to a senior advisory member the next morning; or to answer a question from a six o'clock news reporter. They needed the research to support a vast variety of questions that they had to answer. The one constant was, the research needed to be thorough, accurate and quick. Since the overwhelming majority of us were academics, young lawyers, Ph.D. students or other graduate and postgraduate-level professionals, we were used to doing research and knew how to toggle between two, three and four windows of databases and websites as we worked.

An example of the pace of the work can be illustrated through one of my first research assignments. Brad, an attorney working on the National Security ART, needed information on the second Clinton administration's Domestic Policy Council, National Security Council, and the National Economic Council. He needed to know the organizational structure of the councils; what their functions were; who the key members were; and the scope of their responsibilities. And he needed this information "in a few minutes." Well, he may as well have said he needed it yesterday. I wasn't sure of how to approach the project, so I put on my reference librarian hat and methodically starting searching for information. My initial search was in the Lexis-Nexis database. Too broad. I

narrowed the search to "domestic policy council" and "Clinton Administration" w/s (within the same sentence). I got the names of the council
members of the first administration. Still, too broad. I limited the search
further by date. The hits were more precise, but still not just right. A
few minutes had passed. I asked Noah for help. He assigned two people
to assist me: a young man who seemed afraid of the project, and a young
woman scheduled to get off work soon. The scared young man started
searching and yelled out something about using Wikipedia. I told him
that we needed credible sources, that Wikipedia is a wiki where members
can add and change the information, making the information unreliable.
The young lady suggested using government sites. I agreed. The young
man yelled out, "Google it!" I sighed, knowing that a Google search
would render millions of hits, and then told him to go ahead, knowing
that that would keep him busy and quiet for a while. On her way out, the
young lady suggested that I try searching for "Clinton 4" at www.nara.
gov, the National Archives and Records Administration's website. I tried
searching under "Clinton 4" (which represented the second term, while
"Clinton 2" represented the first). Too broad. I refined the search to
include the search terms "Clinton," "1996," and the name of the council.
Pay dirt! I hit a goldmine of executive orders from the first administration that established the various councils, including their responsibilities,
then switched over to the Lexis-Nexis database to get the names of the
members during the second term. I thanked the young lady and told
Noah that I'd be okay, so that he could pull the young man for another
assignment. Within an hour, I had cut and pasted six pages of information into a final two-page, edited report on each of the three councils!

Quite honestly, if I weren't an information professional, coupled
with being a quick study who could mimic some of the computer short-
cuts that the younger people used, I'm not sure that I could have kept up
with the pace of responsibilities. The right side of the mouse became
my good friend, as did the "send to" arrow button; the "F" function
keys; the control plus the P, V or C keys; and, of course, the old reliable
magic of "cut and paste."

As promised during the campaign, President-Elect Obama intended to hold true to providing more transparency in government – starting with his transition. The transition team was determined to get input from as many people, agencies and organizations from every corner of the nation as possible, and to make those interactions public knowledge. Assisting ARTs with preparing these meeting documents for uploading onto the change.gov website was the third key area where volunteer staff was heavily utilized. The PTT referred to these archived documents as "legacy files." Creating these files involved the following:

- Scanning all meeting documents, i.e., correspondence between individuals or organizations and the PTT, agendas, minutes and participant presentations, in order to convert them from paper to electronic files.

- Emailing the scanned documents (which were now electronic files) to the ART member requesting the work.

- The ART member reviewed the files and forwarded them to the Legal unit.

- Legal reviewed the files and redacted any confidential information, such as personal telephone numbers, cell numbers, and any other non-public information.

- The redacted files were then forwarded to the New Media Department, which converted the electronic files to HTML files that were uploaded to the website.

The array of groups, organizations and concerned citizens that were participating in submitting proposals, ideas and suggestions on how to best tackle the social, economic, environmental, judicial and national security issues that the new administration would face was tremendous. One of the scanning projects that I worked on didn't involve just one ART, but several. The range of groups submitting documents was wide and the topics varied: letters regarding economic policy ideas from Governor Charlie Crist of Florida, the Minority Business Association of Detroit, and the Teamsters; correspondence from groups with social/judicial concerns included Indian associations regarding tribal issues; secularist groups on religious freedom in the military; an Arab-American antidiscrimination group whose concerns were obvious; proposals from engineering consortiums on infrastructure improvements; day care centers on early childhood education issues; and the American Library Association concerned with literacy and digital divide issues for rural communities.

As I scanned and emailed the documents to their corresponding ARTs, I wondered if everyday Americans really understood or knew how labor-intensive (and costly) transparency really was. Were they really willing to pay for it, to pay for the staff and equipment needed? I'd hoped the whole effort was worth it to everybody. One thing for sure, people were involved in a presidential transition and pre-White House administration like never before. So standing at the overheating photocopier/ scanner for hours on end, helping President-Elect Obama fulfill a campaign promise of transparency, made it worth it to me.

Outside of meeting with ARTs, everyday citizens were in contact with the transition in every way possible: written correspondence, call-ins, submitting job applications, and via online comments. But mostly, they mailed in stuff: letters, cards, gifts, and hundreds upon hundreds of books. Upon learning that I was a librarian, Kevin of the mailroom asked for my assistance with cataloguing and processing the overwhelming number of books sent in as gifts to President-Elect and Mrs. Obama, Vice President-Elect Biden, and other key members of the PTT. And as fulfilling as this project was for a librarian, I was still hopeful that this wasn't my assignment outside of the Call Center. I wanted to work with an ART. I was one of the 300,000 job applicants too, and wanted to showcase my skills and capabilities firsthand in an area or department that might be hiring. On December 23rd, as if God himself had heard my prayer, I was notified that I'd been selected to work with the Office of Public Liaison – Religious Outreach.

The Second Month ~
January 2009

Unlike my experience in Denver, this time my travels included temporary lodging with people I actually knew. My best friend Denise's niece and nephew-in-law, Shanise and Wills Allen, opened up their beautiful home in Bristol, Virginia, to me, welcomed me with open arms and delicious home-cooked food. They were a loving family of four, including two bright children, Zhorah in the eighth grade and their sixth-grade son, Sinclair, named for his grandfather, whom I also knew back in the day. Two weeks into my stay in D.C., I'd nabbed a nice one-bedroom apartment, renting it from another PTT volunteer, Robin Kelley. She and her family extended an invitation for me to spend the New Year with them. I declined. I'd spent Christmas Day with her family, and didn't want to impose. I declined an invitation with the Allens as well. I didn't want to impose on them either.

For the first time in years, I was spending the Christmas, Kwanzaa and New Year holidays away from my actual family and close friends. I missed them all terribly. So I lay on the couch in the quiet little apartment and reflected on the past thirty days. I thought about my first day of work at the PTT and of how Wills had taken me under his wing to "show me the ropes" of getting around D.C.; how we'd boarded the Virginia Railway Express (VRE) at the Broad Run Station in Bristol, and as the train whisked along the tracks to downtown D.C., he'd pointed out the local sights: Old Alexandria, the Potomac River, the Pentagon and the Capitol; of how we'd detrained and taken the mile-long walk to D Street, passing the National Mall, the Washington Monument, various museums and the Supreme Court Building along the way. I missed the morning walks and lively conversations with Wills. I missed Shanise's Caribbean cooking of jerk chicken, brown rice and grilled vegetables. The Allens were as close to family that I had in D.C. I missed my mother. I missed my friends. I missed James. The loneliness stung like frostbite. Two things kept me going: James was coming to D.C. soon for the Inauguration events; and after the New Year, I'd start my new assignment with the PTT, working with the Office of Public Liaison – Religious Outreach.

ॐ

"Hi! I'm Mara," a tiny, thirty-something woman with small, soft hands said, extending her hand.

"Hi, Ms. Vanderslice, I'm Michelle Carnes," I responded.

"Oh, please. Call me Mara."

"Okay, Mara. Please call me Michelle."

The Office of Public Liaison and Intergovernmental Affairs was headed by chief counsel Michael Strautmanis. Joshua DuBois was the Director of the Religious Outreach unit. Mara Vanderslice worked with Joshua DuBois. I was assigned to work with Mara.

Even before she introduced herself, I knew exactly who Mara Vanderslice was. I'd done a Google search on her name and image the moment I'd learned of my new assignment. She'd spearheaded the "Matthew 25 Network" PAC (political action committee) for the Obama campaign and was the former director of religious outreach for the Kerry-Edwards campaign in 2004. She was a petite powerhouse of warmth and friendliness who compressed about a day and a half of work into one. On our first day together we hit the ground running.

As the title suggests, the Office of Public Liaison – Religious Outreach focused on garnering policy input from; listening to; and meeting with groups with religious concerns and/or with religious groups of every stripe. My role in assisting with this included the following:

- Contacting participants to either invite them to a meeting or confirm their attendance for a previously arranged meeting;
- Conducting research on all of the meeting participants, condensing the information and providing biographical summaries to be attached to the meeting agendas;
- Meeting, greeting and escorting participants upstairs to the correct conference rooms and later escorting them back downstairs to the security booth afterwards;
- Sitting in on meetings to take notes, if needed;

- And within twenty-four hours of the meetings, scanning all of the meetings' documents to be uploaded into the online legacy files.

This process was fast-paced and ongoing, from early-morning 8 a.m. meetings to after-work 6 p.m. and 7 p.m. meetings. When I wasn't working directly with Mara, I worked with other ARTs that needed assistance. I participated in scores of meetings, calls, escorts and handshakes, two of which especially stand out in my mind: talking to Katrina of the Commission on Preservation of American Heritage Abroad, and meeting with the Faith In Action Working Group.

- On one occasion, I was working with the Space, Science, Technology & Arts Agency Review Team calling various groups and associations to provide policy input from their respective perspectives. One such group was the Commission on Preservation of American Heritage Abroad. This group was involved with helping to preserve sites, memorials, cemeteries and places of worship in Eastern and Central Europe. I called the commission to find out what their interests were and what input would they like to provide to the transition regarding their interests. When I called, an administrative assistant named Katrina answered. When I identified myself as someone from the Obama-Biden Presidential Transition Project, she became so excited that she nearly started crying, ending our conversation with, "We've been here for years and no one from any administration has ever called us or asked for input on anything. My God, how did you even know we were here?"

My exchange with Katrina was indicative of the reaction that most people had when we called and told them that the PTT was calling for their input on a certain matter. How we knew that Katrina's organization existed is because they were a legally registered 501(c)(3) nonprofit. Any organization, no matter how small, if they were a legitimate nonprofit, listed in the telephone book, or listed in the *National Directory of Associations*, they were included in our lists of contacts. Once, when I was part of a team of people calling Native American groups, the listing of names totaled well over five hundred. To illustrate just how small and obscure some of the groups were that we reached out to for the Conservation, Forestry and Lands Issues ART included the following: the Wild Turkey Association, Trout Unlimited, and Pheasants Forever.

On another occasion, when Mara was off sick, she'd asked me to sit in on a meeting with the Faith In Action Working Group and take notes. Joshua DuBois presided over the meeting, and 14 representatives from various organizations attended. Their discussion focused on drugs, drug trafficking, the fair treatment of prisoners, and juvenile delinquents. An overview of the meeting went as follows:

- Joshua opened the meeting with a welcome and explained that the PTT was there to listen; he invited each attendee to make his or her presentation.

- Groups represented at the meeting included: the Sojourners; the Religious Action Center; American Humanist Association; Disciples Center for Public Witness; the General Board of Church and Society; The Mitchell Firm; the Prison Fellowship; the National Alliance of Faith and Justice; Mennonite Central Committee; NAACP of D.C.; United Church of Christ; Founding Church of Scientology of Washington, D.C.; and American Friends Service Committee.

- The first presenter explained that the Faith In Action Working Group was a collective group that represented a membership totaling in the millions; that it was a bipartisan group that worked across political and religious spectrums from the left and right; and that they all agreed that the political justice system needed reform. Subsequent speakers had specific "asks" from their respective groups to the administration that included the following:

  ° Justice Integrity Act: asked the administration to reframe the whole criminal justice problem as a social problem at impacts families, various parts of the community and the larger society; concerned with all areas of the criminal justice system from arrests through sentencing and the over-incarceration of the mentally ill (five times more in prison than in mental health institutions) and African Americans; concerned with prison reform in the areas of treatment of prisoners after arrests; sentencing of prisoners; post-prison treatment; and re-entry of prisoners into the criminal justice system.

- ° Reformation of the "Non-Fraternization Rule": concerned with the administration providing support in the areas of religious rights for prisoners; issues of prison rape; and reforming the rule that prevents religious mentors from staying in touch with prisoners after their release.

- ° Crack/Powder Cocaine Sentencing Disparity: encouraged the administration to focus on the prosecutions of major drug traffickers and retailers and not on low-level drug dealers; and to revise the trigger amounts for sentencing for crack versus powder cocaine by making them 1 to 1 sentencing versus the 20 to 1 sentencing that was currently in place.

- ° Justice and Delinquency Prevention Act: asked that the administration turn the focus to the rehabilitation of delinquent juveniles; remove them from adult jails; provide sight and sound protection for juvenile delinquents; and work on reversing the disproportionate number of African American juveniles in jails.

- ° Fully funding the Second Chance Act: stressed that successful enactment involves integration and cooperation of federal agencies such as the FDA, HUD and Social Security to provide needed social services and mentoring to prevent recidivism.

- ° Democracy Restoration Act: concerned with restoring

federal voting rights to prisoners, which could provide a model for states to follow.

Each presenter spoke as passionately as the last, armed with facts, statistics and dollar amounts to support his or her arguments. Sitting in that room, being witness to and transcriber of citizen participation in government, made me feel wonderfully proud; proud to be a part of the transition; proud to be an open-arms Democrat; proud to be an American.

The next couple of weeks, especially the final one, were a whirlwind of calling people for meetings; providing research on meeting attendees; escorting visitors in and out of the building; vetting donors to make sure they were not lobbyists; cataloguing the multitude of gift books; and carefully packing and closing up shop in preparation for the move over to the White House. The Inauguration was only a few days away, and I'd noticed that neither I nor any of the other volunteers had tickets to any of the events. And then suddenly, on January 14th, Stephanie placed in my hand an invitation to *"please gather in the press briefing room downstairs for a 'thank you' from the transition co-chairs."*

"On behalf of the transition co-chairs, me, Valerie Jarrett (who couldn't be here today) and Pete Rouse, we want to sincerely thank you for all of your hard work," John Podesta said from the podium. "But wait. To bring thanks and greetings from the President-Elect himself is none other than MICHELLE OBAMA!"

The audience of a couple hundred volunteers went wild with cheers and applause. She was a total surprise to us and a welcome treat. She took to the stage and, looking out at all of us standing there, began a heartfelt thank you.

"I want to personally thank you. Barack personally thanks you. We know the sacrifices that you've made to be here. We know that you have traveled from across the nation; left your jobs, schools and families. We know that you all are highly skilled with multiple degrees and are doing the heavy lifting of support work, making calls, making copies, running errands. We know that. And from the bottom of our hearts we thank you for your service to this transition."

I stood with my hands clasped together and my heart full. She was dead on. We had all made quite a sacrifice to be there. The work was fast-paced and at times difficult. It felt good to know that she and her husband knew it and were personally thanking us. I stood at the front of the room on the rope line, looking up, beaming as she spoke. She finished with anecdotal stories of her family's time in Washington, D.C. and their visit with the girls to the Lincoln Memorial. She left the stage and came out into the audience for hand-shaking and picture-taking. She approached me, and I extended my hand.

"Hello, Mrs. Obama," I greeted her. "You know, my name is Michelle, too. I'm working in the Call Center, and people sometimes ask if I'm Michelle Obama."

"Well, I hope you're doing our names proud," she said with a smile.

"Yes Ma'am, I am," I beamed back.

We paused to take a couple of quick photos, which was to be the fourth and last of my photographs with Michelle Obama.

Our spirits were lifted after the "thank you" party. We returned to the Call Center laughing and chatting about what had just taken place, asking who had taken pictures, and swapping email addresses and giving assurances of sharing our respective photographs. In the midst of our buzzing conversations, Stephanie suddenly announced, "Check your emails!" We did, and one by one we began to gasp and scream and laugh and whoop and holler. I nervously, clumsily typed in my email address. A new message was in the inbox, a letter from the PTT HR Department. The subject line read: *Purchase Your Inaugural Ball Tickets Now*.

"Girl, can you believe it!" Robin asked excitedly.

"No, I can't. I mean, yes I can. Oh my God!" I rambled.

"I wonder what made them finally let us get tickets."

"Well, all I can say is, I don't think it was a coincidence that we got a visit from Michelle Obama and on the same day got tickets to the balls."

"Amen," Robin responded.

"Amen, for sure," I repeated.

The Presidential Inauguration Committee (PIC) gave us a one-time, one-shot opportunity to purchase a maximum of four tickets each. Ball tickets were selling from $500 to $1,000, but we could purchase them at a 70 percent discount. I stared at the email in utter disbelief. I reread it and reread it again, then cautiously clicked on the Ticketmaster link to purchase two tickets.

I don't remember walking to the Judiciary Square Metro Station or boarding the train or taking my seat. I was riding on a cloud, my head in a fog. I leaned back in my seat, closing my eyes to relive the day's events. I saw Michelle Obama's wonderful smile and heard her warm words. I saw the lean John Podesta exiting the stage and the humble former private secretary to President Clinton, Betty Currie, clapping as she peeked around the doorway. My mind wandered from that day to the many before, rolling back the film of episodic events and encounters:

- To my first day at the PTT, when Cassandra Butts, General Counsel for the transition team, spoke, smiled and held the door open for me;

- To the time that I walked the hall with Tom Daschle, former South Dakota Senator and nominee for Secretary of Health and Human Services, and we talked about health care reform, with him smiling and complimenting my "GFC – Grassroots Finance Committee" canvas shoulder bag;

- To the lunch break I took in the staff lounge, sitting across from Melody Barnes, Co-Director of Agency Review, and ate as we silently exchanged nods and smiles;

- To the moment I shared a down elevator with Katie Couric of CBS, who made eye contact, smiled and said hello; and once reaching the lobby, encountered Eugene Robinson of the *Washington Post*, talking on a cell phone and getting off of the call to wave and speak to me;

- To seeing a talkative Bill Richardson, Governor of New Mexico, on the first floor and a stern General James Jones, National Security Advisor, on the seventh, to passing a pleasant Christina Romer, Economic Advisor, in the hallway on the ninth;

- To that day when I witnessed a cluster of deaf people chatting in sign language; and blind people being guided through the hallways by determined black Labradors and golden retrievers; and people in battery-powered wheelchairs entering the elevators, swirling around, backing in, making room for more to enter; and a little person not much taller than a small child commanding the attention of people more than twice his height; people with various sorts of disabilities, all smiling and happy and exchanging business cards, pleased at being treated as VIPs by the Obama-Biden PTT staff;

- To the time that a group of us stood outside in the cold, awaiting an "all clear" to re-enter the building, and looking out into the crowd seeing David Axelrod, standing and shivering, talking and waiting, although he wore a special security lapel pin that would have granted him entrance into the building;

- To the time that the Secret Service blocked off the elevators as they barked into their walkie-talkies that "Renegade"[40](Obama) was in the building and on the move.

The cloud of memories accompanied me all the way to my little rental apartment on Capitol Street, and as I sat on the couch dialing James's phone number to give him the good news.

"Get your tux ready, Sweetie!" I shouted into the telephone.

"Why? What's happening?"

"We're going to a presidential inaugural ball!"

"Wow! Which one?"

"The Midwestern Ball, Baby! Wow is right!"

ॐ

INAUGURATION MORNING

"I do solemnly swear (or affirm) that I will faithfully execute the office of the President of the United States, and will to the best of my abil-

---

[40] The code names of the Obama family included: "Renegade" for President-Elect Obama; "Renaissance" for Michelle Obama; "Radiance" for Malia Obama; and "Rosebud" for Sasha Obama. "Obama Family Secret Service Code Names," *Huffingtonpost,* November 10, 2008 [http://www.huffingtonpost.com/2008/11/10/obama-family-secret-servi_n_142767.html].

ity, preserve, protect and defend the Constitution of the United States."[41]

James and I sat in the warm comfort of a bar at the St. Regis Hotel and watched the swearing-in ceremony on a big-screen television. Hours earlier we'd awakened on this January 20th morning at the European-styled Windsor Inn, a small, quaint Art Deco bed-and-breakfast turned independent hotel. We'd shared a morning meal of cold cereal, coffee, pastries, juice and hard-boiled eggs with other hotel guests, including a couple from Brisbane, Australia, who'd traveled to America to be a part of this historic event. In between bites, we all nervously chattered about the unseasonably cold seventeen-degree weather and what we expected President-Elect Obama would say in his upcoming Inaugural Address. As we ate and talked, we also noticed something curious happening – it was eight o'clock on a Tuesday morning and there was no traffic, no automobiles, no buses; just clumps and throes of pedestrians all heading in one direction – towards the National Mall. We finished our coffee and juice, bade our hotel-mates good luck and good-bye and headed out into the frosty D.C. morning to join the waves of fellow patriots in our newly defined march on Washington.

I had secured one "Mall Standing Area - Silver" ticket to the ceremony from the Presidential Inauguration Committee (PIC), and Robin Kelley had unselfishly given me hers so that James could also attend. James and I decided instead to keep our tickets as mementos of this historic day and to view the ceremony from the thick of the crowd with the non-ticketed general public. I was bundled and wrapped in the striped scarf that he had given me a year earlier to take to Iowa, and we began our march.

Despite the chill that hit our throats as we smiled and talked, a heat wave of pride and public ownership of government warmed and filled the air. En route, we walked Sixteenth Street alongside whole families, two to three generations deep, walking and laughing, pausing long enough to pose and snap pictures of themselves, with the surrounding

[41] Every incoming president back to George Washington has spoken these words in the oath of office for the President of the United States. "Where Does the Oath of Office Come From?" NPR Online, January 14, 2009 [http://www.npr.org/templates/story/story.php?storyId=99323353].

crowds and the city as backdrop. We passed old stone structures housing churches, small museums and headquarters of countless national organizations. There were buildings draped in flags, red, white and blue bunting, streamers and blow-up donkeys on the verandas; and advertisements enticing passers-by to come inside to eat, drink, and celebrate this momentous occasion in their establishments. Vendors lined each side of the street for blocks and blocks, as far as the eye could see, selling everything from the frivolous to the necessary, like food and water and hand-and-foot warmers. There were tables and tents of tee-shirts, sweatshirts, skull caps and baseball caps, calendars, refrigerator magnets and framed pictures, all embossed or embroidered with the image and/ or name of the about-to-be-inaugurated President Obama. We stopped to buy a couple of packs of hand warmers, because although there were smiles and sunshine, jubilance and pride in the atmosphere, the wintertime temperature persisted in the upper teens, causing our breath to fog, feet to numb, and fingers to start to tingle.

We followed the crowds that had grown into the thousands and consumed the actual streets of 16th NW and 15th NW and 14th NW that turned onto K Street NW and towards Independence Avenue NW, until the mouth of the National Mall was visible. We entered the mall, cutting across crunching grass beneath our feet, past the Reflecting Pond solid in some places, not frozen in others, where it faintly cast shadows of the barren trees and brick buildings nearby; past rows and rows of people bundled in suede coats with sheep shearing, old men in leather bomber jackets and knit baseball caps, small children in mittens and winter boots holding tightly onto the gloved hands of their mothers. We captured these movements and moments on film, James with a color-film camera, me with a black-and-white. We walked along, drinking in the sights and sounds of the moment, flanked by the majestic Washington Monument obelisk to the east and the massive Jefferson Memorial to our west; turning and snapping pictures, stopping and posing for photos of ourselves, greeting and laughing with strangers, and smiling at the corps of red-shirted volunteers guiding us towards the many jumbotrons that had been erected around the Mall to satellite the broadcast of the day's events.

Slowly, respectfully we walked through the flagged and circular open-air structure of the WWII Memorial, pausing long enough to touch the marble markers and to read their inscriptions; quietly exiting that place and journeying on to the top of a small mound where we stood and turned, looking behind us at the thousands of faces of every race and complexion imaginable, tight with determination, steeled against the below-freezing temperature, beaming with pride.

James looked happy, but cold, and, for whatever manly reason, refused to put hand warmers inside of his gloves. His lips, usually a soft pink, had turned a weird shade of faint purple. We took the last of our pictures among the crowds, before deciding that our fifty-plus-year-old bodies would fare better indoors, in the warmth, perhaps with a hot drink of something in our hands. So we backtracked our steps, past the Hay Adams Hotel where the Obamas had stayed when refused residence at the Blair House by the Bush Administration; and on to the St. Regis Hotel, where a sidewalk sign welcomed us in for a viewing of the presidential swearing-in ceremony and Inauguration Address.

"My fellow citizens: I stand here today humbled by the task before us, grateful for the trust you've bestowed, mindful of the sacrifices borne by our ancestors.

"That we are in the midst of crisis is now well understood. . . Today I say to you that the challenges we face are real. They are serious and they are many. They will not be met easily or in a short span of time. But know this America: They will be met.

"On this day, we gather because we have chosen hope over fear, unity of purpose over conflict and discord. On this day, we come to proclaim an end to the petty grievances and false promises, the recriminations and worn-out dogmas that for far too long have strangled our politics. We remain a young nation. But in the words of Scripture, the time has come to set aside childish things. The time has come to reaffirm our enduring spirit; to choose our better history; to carry forward that precious gift, that noble idea passed on from generation to generation; the God-given promise that all are equal, all are free, and all deserve a chance to pursue their full measure of happiness.

"Let it be said by our children's children that when we were tested we refused to let this journey end, that we did not turn back nor did we falter; and with eyes fixed on the horizon and God's grace upon us, we carried forth that great gift of freedom and delivered it safely to future generations.

"Thank you. God bless you. And God bless the United States of America."[42]

And just as now-President Obama spoke his last words, the waitstaff of the St. Regis, standing at the ready with bottles of champagne in hand, popped the corks. Corks flew through the air like little missiles, making loud popping sounds in the process. Champagne bubbled over and ran down the sides of the bottles as the waitstaff swiftly wiped it away and began filling our awaiting glasses. We raised our champagne flutes in a toast to the new president. The time had finally come to celebrate.

※

INAUGURATION NIGHT

Up to and including this point, my involvement in the campaign, the transition, and now the inauguration activities had been a mixture of part journey, part history, and part collection of awesome memories. This night, however, began a great fairy tale. And just as Cinderella's story includes a fabulous ball near the end, so does mine.

James fastened the clasp of the crystal bead choker I'd chosen to wear with my black mesh and sequin form-fitting evening gown. He donned his custom-fitted band tuxedo and the shirt that he'd given me to wear during the nomination acceptance speech in Denver. In preparation for the cold of the night air, we'd bundled in winter coats, hiking boots and the ever-present gray striped scarf atop our after-five finery. That night was ripe with memories, down to the clothes we wore, clothes that had been part-and-parcel of this journey since the beginning. We

---

[42] Excerpts from the transcript by Macon Phillips, "President Barack Obama's Inaugural Address," *The White House Blog*, January 21, 2009 [http://www.whitehouse.gov/blog/inaugural-address/].

walked through the hotel vestibule, past Ms. Africa USA, who looked absolutely stunning in a flesh-tone and black lace strapless evening gown that blossomed into a cascade of lace and sequin ruffles; past the lineup of taxicabs at the curb near the hotel steps; down the buzzing sidewalks of U Street and onward to the U Street/African American Civil War Memorial/Cardozo Metro Station on the green line.

We held hands and rode in silence to our stop, anticipating the excitement of the evening and observing the other passengers on the train: a young black couple, the woman in powder blue chiffon and silver, escorted by a tall, slender Army officer in full-dress uniform, holding onto a train rail with one hand and dangling his date's silver sling-back shoes in the other; a web of giggling women in short dresses and long overcoats, spike-heeled boots and swanky updo hair; a thirty-something woman and a small child sitting next to her staring in amazement; an older white couple, the women in stoic navy blue and pearls, the man in a tight tuxedo and ponytail. We occasionally looked over at one another and smiled, before getting off at the Mt. Vernon Square/7th Street–Convention Center stop.

We exited into the night. Even above the cold, we could feel something special in the air. It was inauguration night in the nation's capital! Downtown D.C. hummed with crowds of people, dressed in smiles and finery, looking like adults out on a grown-ups prom. We walked with the parade of crowds across 6th Street, over to 7th Street, making our way to New York Avenue and on to the Washington Convention Center. I clutched the handbag that held our tickets to the Midwestern Ball close to my chest and racing heart. The Midwestern Ball was just one of ten official presidential inaugural balls. This ball would include people from Kansas, Indiana, Iowa, Michigan, Wisconsin, Missouri and the Dakotas. I smiled at the thought of maybe seeing some of the people I'd worked with in Iowa, or walked the streets with in Indiana. Maybe I'd get to see and chat with Tom Daschle again, or get a firsthand glimpse of the First Couple dancing at midnight. *Maybe this was all a dream, a wonderful dream,* I thought. A breeze of chilling night air stroked my face. No, this was not a dream. It only felt like it.

"So, fee-fi-fo-fum! Look out baby, 'cause here I come!
And I'm bringing you a lo-ove that's tr-true.
So get read-dy! So get read-dy! 'Cause here I come!"

We walked in on a brassy rendition of the Fabulous Motown Revue kicking off the evening, belting out one of the Temptations' famous songs. The large, fifteen- or sixteen-piece band decked out in black tie and white satin, appropriately for the Midwestern Ball was from St. Louis, Missouri. The huge ballroom was elegant, formal and patriotic, decorated in gold drapes at each end of the two stages, light gray carpet covering the concrete convention hall floors underneath, soft amber track lighting near the ceiling, and with gold, blue and white inauguration seals and flags on the walls throughout. We stood at the edge of the dance floor, rocking to the bass sounds of the band as we watched the couples dance. Old couples, middle-aged couples, black couples, white couples, clumps of college-aged women, all swaying and swinging in beat with the tunes. Laughter and gaiety filled the air, mixing in with the mingled scents of beer, wine, grilled chicken and vegetables. We made our rounds hitting the food stations, sampling pâté-filled pastries, spring rolls, penne pasta, cheese squares and chicken strips. We walked through the massive ballroom sipping Riesling and White Zinfandel wines, meeting new people, taking pictures and asking them to take photos of us. We joined the others on the dance floor, as the vigorous band singers piped out the Supremes' *"You Keep Me Hangin' On"* and Marvin Gaye's *"What's Going On"* in the background. Magic and love and happiness and soulful sounds filled the room.

The band slowly, quietly stopped playing. A sudden hush filled the room. Lights over the stage at the opposite end of the room rose. Out walked the petite and beautiful pop/rock/folk singer Sheryl Crow, also from Missouri. The room exploded into applause and shouts. She smiled and began singing, captivating the crowd with her version of the old Cat Stevens tune *"The First Cut Is The Deepest."*

James and I absorbed the music, our bodies moving to its rhythm and beat. We worked our way across the dance floor, over to the emptied stage and sat at its edge. Sheryl Crow moved into a performance of Johnny Nash's *"I Can See Clearly Now."* A lone couple slow-danced beneath a disco ball of sparkling stars, the woman lean and graceful in a flowing white gown, the man commanding yet careful as he twirled her just so, causing her sequined gown to reflect bits of the golden stars dancing high above them. I held onto James's hand and looked overhead at the swirling stars. The man I admired had become president. The man I loved was there to share the moment. The melodious Sheryl Crow crooned in the background. The night was winding down. And just like in the Cinderella fairy tale, the midnight hour was approaching and the time to go home had come.

Arm in arm, James and I walked across the star-studded dance floor and towards the door. I paused for one last time to soak in the sounds and sights and memories of the night, and was filled to the brim with joy. *No, this isn't a dream,* I thought. *It only feels like it.*

Me working the phones; Noah and Stephanie (PTT Call Center Managers) stopped for a quick pose; and Robin Kelley is all smiles as she and other Health Care Team members worked the numbers during the early efforts for national health care.

Me and the future First Lady after she spoke to and thanked the
PTT staff in D.C.

My Official PTT Badge.

My friends Denise, Rosalyn, Cheryl and Diretha looking over my scrapbook
after my return from working the PTT.

James and I danced the night away at the Midwestern Inaugural Ball,
January 20, 2009.

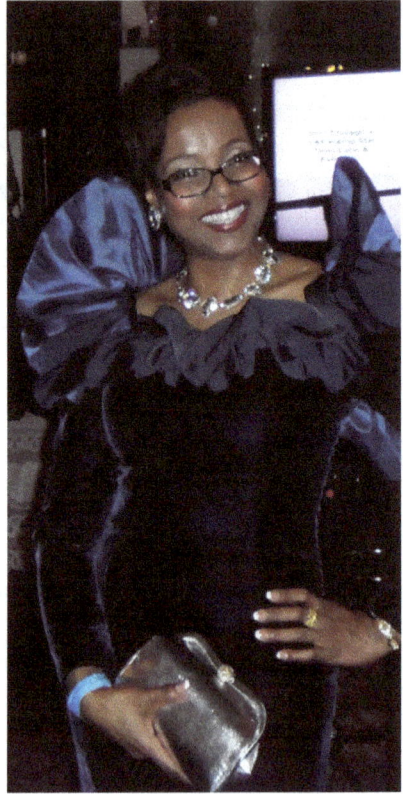

Four years later, my sister Debra and I are decked out for the
2013 Inaugural Ball!

Debra and Robin after th
2013 Inauguration Swea
ing-In Ceremony.

CHAPTER

Eight

THE END OF A FANTASTIC RIDE

The Journey Ends

"Any word yet on when the train will be here?" I asked the ticket agent for the third time.

"No update yet, Ma'am. Situation's the same. We'll let you know, okay?"

"Yeah. Thanks," I mumbled as I walked away.

I rejoined James at the little table round we'd staked out as we waited in the Albany-Rensselaer train station. Thumbing through a *New Yorker* magazine, he absently drank a beer and hunched his shoulders slightly as I relayed the "no change" update on the status of our train. He was being quiet. That meant he was upset. And with good reason, too: we were five hours into waiting for the mechanically delayed train to arrive from Penn Station. I went outside for a smoke and to get some air. Leaning against the outdoor railings, I recounted the events that had gotten us here.

The trip had started out smoothly enough, filled with groggy excitement and the anticipation of returning home.

"All aboard! Amtrak train number 172 now boarding!"

The conductor's voice boomed above the early-morning commuting noise of cars, pedestrians, buses, cabs and train horns; all moving and bustling to get people off to work, or to the gym, or to a coffee shop, or like us, departing D.C. to return to our normal lives back home. We'd arisen at four in the morning and raced around as much as one can at that hour and on such little sleep, showering, packing five suitcases, double-checking that we hadn't left anything behind, hailing a cab and finally joining the line of creepy-crawly rush-hour traffic. We walked through beautiful Union Station, admiring its old world architecture of tall ceilings, arched doorways and stone staircases, on through to the loading area. We entered the business class section of the Northeast Regional train, taking it all the way to the end of the line, to New York Penn Station – the first leg of our long way home.

I settled back into my seat, the hot coffee and anticipation of the trip waking me up. Our train route back home was a convoluted one, because like the hundreds of thousands of other people who'd come to partake in the inauguration events, we were all at the same time heading back to our respective neighborhoods. Available non-stop flights and trains from D.C. to Chicago were non-existent. So we were taking the *Northeast Regional* from D.C. to New York Penn Station, then on to the *Empire Service* train from Penn Station to Albany, New York, and finally onto the *Lake Shore Limited* from Albany to Chicago that would get us back home by nine o'clock the next day. I sipped coffee and looked out the window, as the train sailed out of D.C. and into Prince George's County, Maryland; through Baltimore and onward; through the industrial cities of Delaware, making the same station stop in Wilmington that Vice President Biden had exited for thirty-six years. The train glided smoothly along the tracks, continuing on through rustic Philadelphia with its narrow rowhouses and centuries-old stone buildings; through Trenton and Newark, New Jersey; until finally we reached New York City, Penn Station, where we realized we didn't have baggage stubs for the five pieces of luggage that we'd checked back in D.C.

The ride between New York City and Albany was just under three captivatingly scenic hours of curvaceous countryside along the Hudson River Valley. The quiet train car of a handful of passengers coasted along the tracks, paralleling the Harlem and Hudson rivers; passing through the metropolis of New York City and on to the hills of Yonkers; through Irvington, so named for its famous author, Washington Irving of *Rip Van Winkle* and *The Legend of Sleepy Hollow* storybook fame; past the historic Bannerman's Castle and Catskills mountains; through Dutch-settled

Poughkeepsie and up the river on to the hamlet of Rhinecliff; until lastly we reached our destination of Albany, the capital of all of New York. By the time we detrained, James was telling stories of that portion of his boyhood spent living in Albany, back when his father was in the early stages of becoming a pediatrician. We'd forgotten about our baggage problem, too consumed in remembrances and walking down memory lane. We looked forward to the last leg of our trip and stretching out in a sleeper car. And now this, an indefinite wait on an indeterminate fix to a train with an unknown arrival time.

"Hey. Let's walk," James said solemnly, as he sidled next to me, interrupting my thoughts.

We walked atop the snow-packed sidewalks bordering the train station, down a slight decline, up an ice-patched incline, following the curves of the road until we turned the corner; passing by a bar closed up for the night and accompanying pizza shop pulling its blinds. We rounded another corner and another until the Dutch-styled neighborhood near the station, complete with a small church with a tall, snow-capped steeple, was in sight. We re-entered the station. Boxes of hot pizzas and two-liter bottles of soft drinks were stacked on the small waiting room tables. They were feeding us. That was not a good sign.

Thirteen hours into waiting for the delayed train to reach Albany, it arrived. My body screamed with aches and pains after hours of trying to sleep on the hard, lumpy station room chairs. We slowly, wearily dragged our feet and carry-on bags out of the waiting room and onto the loading area, up the short flight of stairs to the top floor of the train, down the narrow hallway and on to our sleeper compartment. We entered the small room, called a roomette, a place no larger than a walk-in closet with just enough space for two bags and two bunk beds. I wanted to scream, but disappointment, frustration and weariness held it back. I reluctantly climbed up to the top bunk, kicked off my shoes, loosened my jeans and closed my eyes. A toddler across the hall let out a rattling scream, followed by another one and then another one, screaming as hard and loudly as her two-year-old lungs could muster. I lay awake in the dark sleeper looking out at a black sky and distant stars. Just 24 hours earlier,

I'd been dancing on soft carpeting under golden stars. Another bellow-ing scream. *Perfect*, I thought, an apropos punctuation to a train trip that had slowly descended into a train wreck.

ᔥ

Our five pieces of luggage were waiting when we arrived at Union Station in Chicago. We were twelve hours behind schedule and looked every bit of it; slept-in, wrinkled and rumpled clothes that had been worn for over 24 hours, hair with no curls, dulled makeup, in need of more breath mints.

"Hey James! Hey Michelle!" Mike cheerily greeted us with a big hug. "Wow. What in the world happened to y'all?"

And after more than 24 hours of no showers, we probably smelled every bit of it too.

We looked at him and looked at ourselves, then let out a laugh before quickly filling him in on the horrors of the train trip. We were tired and unattractive, but it felt good being back home, seeing a familiar face. Mike's wife, my homey Denise, would be waiting in the car. I could hardly wait to see her. The three of us made our way up the escalators and out into the Chicago winter air. It was freezing out, but that was okay as well. The train trip was behind us, and we were in our beloved hometown. Denise got out of the idling SUV and we embraced for a long time, holding each other close and tight, transmitting the warmth of more than thirty-five years of history and love and friendship between us, until the chilling temperature forced us inside the car.

James and I sat in the back seat. I leaned back and looked up through the sunroof at the night sky, letting my mind wander. It had been nearly two years to the date, back on January 24, 2007, when I first wrote a check and got involved in the Obama presidential campaign. I thought about the crazy calls at the National Headquarters and the snow-covered walkways of Iowa from a year ago; about the campaign video shoot in late July, the one of me standing near the tall granite columns in the beautifully serene Cancer Survivors Garden on Randolph Street encour-aging others to give money and get involved in the campaign, the one where I'd been hand-picked by Chris Hughes to be the spokesperson for the Grassroots Finance Committee. I thought about the thrill of being at the mile-high stadium during the national convention in Denver; about the long, hot walks along the aging and desolate streets of Gary, Indiana; about the summertime parade in Crestwood, Illinois, marching proudly with Mickey's daughter, Melanie Sammons, and her friend Ashley Dieudonne as we carried a "Yes We Can" banner; about the rustic colors of autumn on Halloween night with fiery candidate Obama in Highland, Indiana; and about the unseasonably clement election night in The Big Bar at the Hyatt Hotel. These, just as many other remembrances of the countless up-and-down episodes of the campaign and transition, rushed to my mind. And I realized that through them all, at every turn, James had been there. For nearly all of my time spent involved in the campaign, he'd been there supporting, encouraging, advising and comforting me. And again, tonight, here he sat.

I grabbed his hand and held it tightly. Mike commanded the wheel, slicing through the sleepy nighttime traffic with ease. Denise sat on the passenger side, humming along, slightly ahead of the song on the radio. Our guy had won, and I'd done my part in making that happen. We all had, by holding onto faith and promise and hope and dreams. I wasn't sure where my road ahead would lead, but it looked promising. The time had now come to do something that I hadn't done for nearly two years – lay down my armor and rest, sleep, dream. At last my journey had ended, and I was heading home.

❧

AFTERWORD

Two thousand and twelve was much like history repeating itself. The country could just as well have been set in 1912, where the sons and daughters of the Gilded-Age industrialist lived large in big hats, big jewels, long cars, titanic cruise liners. This time, however, the sons of the robber baron pack would be led by Mitt Romney. President Obama, on the other hand, often compared to Presidents Lincoln and Kennedy, to me resembles the progressive environmentalist of a hundred years ago – President Theodore Roosevelt. So, with the Main Street populous messages of "income redistribution" and "healthcare for all" coming from President Obama on one side, and the Wall Street venture capitalist mantra from former Bain Capital president Mitt Romney on the other, the presidential campaign this go-round boiled down to three very important words: *takers versus makers.*

While this lopsided financial landscape was taking form, so was the ugly face of voter suppression. In 2012, GOP lawmakers were busy and quite blatant in their decisions to disenfranchise the vote of blacks, women and young people – as if the 15th, 19th and 26th amendments had never happened. New voter suppression laws were being mandated across America, particularly in the Old South states like Florida and North Carolina, out west in Arizona and throughout the heartland in Pennsylvania, Ohio and Wisconsin. All of these states made voting more difficult, if not almost impossible for some, by changing election laws to now include new government-sanctioned IDs, which did not include college-issued IDs because college students were no longer considered "real" residents of the towns, cities and precincts in which they resided; to cutting the number of days voters could cast early votes; to eliminating early voting altogether; to shortening the hours of voting on Election Day. And for added insurance, in case any of these tactics didn't work, the granddaddy tactic of them all was used – gerrymandering districts to ensure that one party and only one party, the Republican Party, won those districts.

After the hard-fought election of 2008 and excitement of the Inauguration afterward, I along with millions of other volunteers and voters needed rest. So we did. And like the fabled Rip Van Winkle, we rested and slept – a bit too deeply and much too long. We slept straight through the 2010 midterm election and woke up to what President Obama described as a good old-fashioned "shellacking." The Republicans had commandingly taken back the House of Representatives, which now included an influx of ultra-conservative Tea Party Republicans poised to oppose the president and their own party at every turn.

The defeat was shocking, unsettling and as painful as an elephant sitting on my chest. The time had come to strap on my OFA armor and begin the second phase of my involvement in the Obama presidential campaigns.

Again I worked at the OFA National Headquarters (NHQ). This time it was housed in the historic Prudential Building on Michigan Avenue. The abundant headquarters occupied an entire floor, filled with wall-to-wall windows that exposed the blue-green curves of Lake Michigan at one end and the tall steel shadows of downtown skyscrapers at the other. Like before, me and a few other hand-picked gray hairs worked in the Call Center, while a much larger contingency of young people held down other departments. The young people were younger, smarter, more tech-savvy and more determined. The truth is we all were more determined. The stakes were higher and the opponent much more elusive. Mitt Romney was a nondescript, hard-to-like, seemingly empty suit with deep pockets. If Romney had been the only opponent, that wouldn't have been much of a battle, because the base of his own party viewed him as a blueblood snob who wasn't conservative enough for their liking (or votes). But we weren't just fighting Romney. We were up against big-moneyed political action committees (PACs), deep-pocketed billionaires, a bigoted Republican base and a Senate minority leader who had vowed to make President Obama a one-term president. It was going to take a lot of hard work, something short of a miracle and a billion dollars to win this race – all of which happened over the hard-fought months leading up to the November 6th election.

Over the course of those months, missteps were made, truths were revealed, mounds of money was raised, momentum shifted, Mother Nature intervened, voters doggedly stood in hours-long lines until in the end, a president was elected. Some of the more memorable episodes during that time included the following:

ROMNEY'S "WHITE ELEPHANT" CAMPAIGN

- **The real Romneys were exposed.** Mitt and Ann Romney became synonymous with the über-wealthy characters on *Gilligan's Island*, Mr. and Mrs. Thurston Howell III. Through their own doings, they proved to be far removed from the realities of the everyday working man and woman and, hence, unelectable.

- **Dressage.** Ann Romney's prized horse Rafalca, which doubled as a "business expense," was flown to London to compete in the dressage competition during the Summer Olympics. This didn't sit well with a base filled with blue-collar workers that had never heard of the French term *dressage*, which roughly translates to mean "horse ballet."

- **Home Improvement.** An expensive and ill-timed construction of a car elevator to the interior of one of the Romneys' West Coast mansions took place during a time when the construction of homes was at a standstill and home foreclosures for millions of Americans was on the rise.

- **Campaign Sound Bites.** From Mitt Romney's insistence that "corporations are people too," to his suggestion of "self deportation" for solving the illegal immigration problem; to his caught-on-tape declaration during a $50,000-per-plate fundraiser that *"47% of Americans believe that they are victims, are entitled to health care, food and housing, and will never take personal responsibility and care for their lives"*[43] were all campaign comments that embarrassed the Republican elite and disheartened the

---

[43] Full transcript of Mitt Romney's comment is available in *Mother Jones* online magazine, September 12, 2012 at: http://www.motherjones.com/politics/2012/09/full-transcript-mitt-romney-secret-video.

party's base and Republican-leaning Independents.

Just as Mitt Romney began turning off the working class members of the Republican base, other Republican men simultaneously began turning off women:

- **Rush Limbaugh.** In February 2012, Rush Limbaugh, the radio shock jock deemed as the unofficial leader of the Republican Party, unapologetically referred to Sandra Fluke (a Georgetown law student who spoke on the subject of employer insurance coverage for contraception during an unofficial hearing held by House Democrats) as a "slut" who was having so much sex that she couldn't afford to pay for her contraception. His comments that initially hailed triumphant later proved to be very damaging to the Republican Party through the eyes of single women voters.

- **Bob McDonnell.** In March 2012, Governor Bob McDonnell of Virginia initially supported a bill that would have required that a woman undergo a transvaginal ultrasound procedure at least 24 hours before having an abortion, but ended up signing a bill that required a woman to have a transabdominal ultrasound procedure instead. Within months after signing the bill into law, Governor McDonnell became known as "Governor Vaginal Probe," a negative image that followed him throughout the rest of his term.

- **Todd Akin.** During a local television interview on August 19, 2012, Missouri senatorial candidate Todd Akin broadened the divide between women and Republicans with his ill-informed comment about "legitimate rape" by stating, "*. . .If it's a legitimate rape, the female body has ways to try to shut the whole thing down.*"[44] Todd Akin lost his election to the Democratic candidate, Senator Claire Mc-Caskill.

- **Richard Mourdock.** Right on the heels of Todd Akin's comment, another senatorial candidate, Richard Mourdock of Indiana, said the following: "*. . .And even when life begins in that horrible situation of*

---

[44] The full Todd Akin interview during the taping of *The Jaco Report* on Fox 2 television is available online at: http://fox2now.com/2012/08/19/the-jaco-report-august-19-2012/.

rape, that it is something that God intended to happen."[45] Mr. Mourdock's scorching comment cleaved even more women from the Republican Party. Mr. Mourdock lost his election to the Democratic candidate Joe Donnelly.

- **Mitt Romney.** And finally, as if to drive the last nail into the proverbial coffin, Mitt Romney added his voice to an already tone-deaf chorus of Republican men who didn't seem to understand, value, or respect women. During the second presidential debate in October, in a botched statement intended to be a compliment about the vast number of qualified women ready to fill White House cabinet positions, Romney said the following: *"And we took a concerted effort to go out and find women who had backgrounds that could be qualified to become members of our cabinet. I went to a number of women's groups and said: 'Can you help us find folks,' and they brought us whole binders full of women."*[46] The "binders full of women" comment immediately went viral on Twitter and was transformed into parodies on YouTube and SNL. But beneath the laughter was anger and resentment. The sense that the GOP just didn't get, or perhaps didn't even like women, stuck in the minds of women straight through November and into Election Day.

Other events such as the ill-fated improvisation by an aged Clint Eastwood during the Republican National Convention, talking to an empty chair that was intended to represent and insult President Obama, ended up making the GOP look small and petty. And once the president's immediate tweet of a photo of his chair in the Oval Office along with the caption, *"This seat is taken,"* went viral, the laughter could be heard around the world. Coupled with the Democrats' growing anger over and resistance to the voter suppression laws that were being enacted; to Mitt Romney's offensive "47%" and "self-

---

[45] Video of Mr. Mourdock's comment during a senatorial debate on Oct. 23, 2012 is available on CBS News Online at: http://www.cbsnews.com/news/richard-mourdock-even-pregnancy-from-rape-something-god-intended/.

[46] The full transcript and video of the Oct. 16, 2012 presidential debate are available online via *The New York Times* at: http://www.nytimes.com/interactive/2012/10/17/us/politics/20121017-second-presidential-debate-obama-romney.html?_r=0.

deportation" comments; to the late-October super-storm Sandy that devastated the states of New York and New Jersey and caused Republican Governor Chris Christie to lock arms with and heap praise on to President Obama; just as with women voters, African Americans, Hispanics and young voters, Republican-leaning Independents began rethinking and retreating and quietly lining up to vote for President Obama.

THE OBAMA WIN AND THE KARMA OF 47%

In the end, President Barack Obama was overwhelmingly reelected with just over 51% of the popular vote, beating Mitt Romney with 332 to 206 Electoral College votes.[47] Ironically, poetically even, Romney lost the presidency by garnering a fraction above 47% of the vote. Republicans were blindsided by Romney's loss. From the plutocrats down to the hourly worker, none of them seemed to comprehend that Mitt Romney and his Draconian economic policies were not something that the majority of Americans wanted. The billionaire donors were first stunned, then outraged at the millions upon millions of dollars they'd wasted on an empty campaign. The technocrats of Romney's campaign had gotten the demographic numbers wrong. The field operatives had underestimated the pushback against the GOP voter suppression tactics. The candidate's lackluster performance during the campaign had dampened an already tepid base, suppressing the voter turnout totals on his side. Until consequently, Mitt Romney, the famed Bain Capital "numbers guy," just couldn't make the numbers work.

The money numbers weren't on the Republicans' side either. The threat of tens of millions of dollars being donated to his campaign by a handful of billionaires should have been enough to make Democrats cower. It didn't. Instead, through the collective might of millions of small donors, Democrats raised the billion dollars needed to win. As reported by Open Secrets, a research group that tracks dollars raised and spent on politics, Democrats raised over $1.1 billion to the Republicans' more than $1.2 billion. Having raised enough money to win was only part of the story,

---

[47] 2012 Presidential Election vote totals and breakdowns are available on CNN's *Election Center* online site at: http://www.cnn.com/election/2012/results/main.

though. Turning out the vote was the other. Based on CNN's 2012 Election Day exit polling and a 2013 Census Bureau analytical report titled "The Diversifying Electorate," this is how President Obama won: 93% of African Americans voted for President Obama, 6% for Romney; 73% vs. 26% of Asians; 71% vs. 27% of Hispanics; 60% vs. 37% of young people ages 18-29; and 55% vs. 44% of women. Mitt Romney carried the white and male votes by 59% and 52%, respectively, to President Obama's 39% and 44%.[48]

Reelecting the president in 2012 was a tougher fight with more at stake. The legacy of his presidency and the continuation of his progressive legislative agenda for women and families, education, climate change, prison reform, immigration reform, wage reform and pay equity were all on the line. The battle to keep the White House was fought on several fronts, from standing up to standing in long lines; to acting up; to raising our voices and raising money; to the data scientists crunching the numbers to know where the voters were; to the field operatives who knocked on doors and tapped into the emotions of the people on the other side of those doors; to the voters who stood up for their franchisement by taking seats in portable chairs as they waited in blocks-long lines to cast their votes; to the pure grit, will, determination and pride that was balled up in each and every one of us who were willing to withstand whatever it took to make history this one last time. And history was made. Not only in the reelecting of the nation's first African American president, but because no other president since Dwight D. Eisenhower had ever been elected two times in a row with over 51% of the vote.[49]

Till this day, friends ask was the victory of the second election different from the first. Yes, I answer. Victory this time was not only sweet, but was a validation of Obama's presidency and vindication of his vision and leadership. They ask do I still believe in President Obama. Again, I answer yes. I don't always agree with his decisions, but do trust

[48] Detailed exit polling is available at: http://www.cnn.com/election/2012/results/race/president# from CNN and at: www.census.gov/prod/.../p20-568.pdf from the U.S. Census Bureau.

[49] As reported in several news sources, including Bloomberg News at: http://www.bloomberg.com/news/2013-01-03/final-tally-shows-obama-first-since-56-to-win-51-twice.html.

and believe in his long-term vision. I'm proud of and grateful for Obamacare. I helped fight for that. I'm pleased with his courage to stand up for women and immigrants and the LGBT community. I'm happy that under his steady hand, the economy is bouncing back and that all of my friends and relatives who were unemployed a few years ago are once again among the working. In a nutshell, I'm proud of this president and proud of the role that I've played in getting him both elected and reelected. And when the history of these campaigns is written, I want the voices of the personal histories of the millions of us who made these elections possible to be part of the story being told.

It's been five years between the time that I wrote about the 2008 campaign and now. During that time, many things in my personal life have also changed:

- My mother is doing well, and although she has the normal aches, pains and complaints of anyone else in their late seventies, she's active in church, still dresses to the nines, enjoys working in her garden and playing bingo on Fridays.

- My sister Debra and I attended the 2013 Inauguration ceremonies and ball together. Instead of dancing under the stars of strobe lights as I did during the first Inauguration, she and I were the stars of the ball as we smiled and danced and giggled the way we did as happy little girls.

- My best friends, Denise and Rosalyn, and I still get together for our regular "girls night out" where we take in a movie and occasionally laugh too loud during dinner afterward. And although Denise is experiencing some health issues, her family, her husband Mike, Rosalyn and I are right by her side every step of the way.

- Thanks to my nephew Eddie and his wife Keisha, I now have two more nieces – Eden Renee and Emeri Rose – to whom this book is also dedicated.

- And lastly, James got married – just not to me. We're no longer in touch, but I wish him the best in his new life. As for me, when the time and man are right, I know marriage will happen in my life, too.

And so, here's where it ends. This is the complete story of my involvement in both of the Barack Obama presidential campaigns. It's such a blessing to have been one of the threads connecting the wonderfully exotic fabric of America's political quilt. I'm often asked if I'll get involved in a Hillary Clinton presidential campaign if she decides to run in 2016. Her election, too, would be historic, making her the first woman president. Will she run? Will I be a part of that history if she does? Only time will tell what either of us will do.

⚬

ACKNOWLEDGMENTS

Transforming personal journal entries, memories, photos and life-changing experiences into a published book is not a quick and easy jaunt, but rather a long and winding journey that takes its own sweet time to complete. That's what writing this book has been for me, and along the way, several key people have encouraged, supported, cajoled, suggested, insisted, reminded or patiently waited until my disjointed thoughts could be spun into a story worth reading. I'd like to take this opportunity to thank each of them.

The thought of writing a book about my campaign experience was born from a conversation I had a few years back with Dr. Misbahudeen Admed-Rufai, then chairperson of the Social Science Department and professor of American, African American and African History at Harold Washington College. Upon learning that I'd been a part of the Obama-Biden Transition Team, he declared, *"You must write about this!"* While I was content with simply having my journals and photos to share with my great-nieces when they got old enough to talk politics, Dr. Rufai was not. Each time he'd see me at a college-wide meeting or visited the library, he asked, *"Have you written your book yet?"* I'd embarrassingly answer no. To which he'd respond, *"You must write your book!"* This continued for months. I wasn't writing the book, but the seed had been planted, and my answer to his question had become *not yet.* Several more months passed before I could proudly declare to Dr. Rufai that I was finally writing the book. To which he responded with a loud, hearty laugh and said, *"Good! I wish to read it when it's published."* I wish to publicly thank Dr. Rufai for his relentless insistence that I turn my personal story into a public one for others to share in and hopefully to learn from. He will be amongst the first to receive a copy of the published book.

When I shared with James, my boyfriend at the time, the conversation with Dr. Rufai, he smiled and simply said, *"I agree. You should write a book."* I finally agreed to write it, only if he'd agree to edit it and give an honest critique. I wish to thank him for not only editing the seventh draft of my manuscript, making it presentable enough to give to a publisher, but for working the campaign and keeping me strong through its ups and downs.

I owe hugs, kisses and many thanks to my friends and family who supported me throughout the campaign and in this endeavor. To my sister, Debra, who encouraged me on several occasions to keep going on the campaign and to continue with writing the book. And who, upon first hearing the stories from my journal entries, either laughed or wept and would always end with, *"Read it again."* To my brother Calvin and Aunt Ellen, both of whom supported me with love and donations and expressions of pride. To my longtime BFF, Denise Snyder, who gave my first fundraising party when I was a member of the OFA Grassroots Fundraising Committee; to volunteering her time in the Call Center and along with her husband Mike canvassing the streets of Gary, Indiana; to being there to see me off at the train station for my trip to D.C.; to along with Mike, being there to pick me upon my return. To my other longtime college BFF, Rosalyn "Mickey" Jamison, who tirelessly supported the campaign through volunteering, fundraising, canvassing and enlisting her friends and family to do the same. And who carefully read the edited manuscript and offered great suggestions that made the writing more fluid. To my coworkers Todd Heldt, Don Baird, Versie Barnes and Sherry Ledbetter for working the campaign whenever I asked and for covering at work when I needed the time off. To all of these wonderful people who supported me when they could have easily said no, I say thank you.

To Dr. Dennis J. Woods and his wife, Chantia, a manuscript is just that until a publisher decides to invest his time, skill, energy and resources into churning it into a book. For that, I thank you both for guiding me through the editing and publishing process, but mostly for believing in my book enough to put your imprint on it.

Lastly, and most importantly, I wish to thank my mother, Doris Levy.

Who long before I ventured into the Obama campaign, had been there to support me; who laid a foundation of love on which I could plant my feet and grow; who was the first to support me in my support of President Obama and the last to lie down and rest at night, worrying over whether I'd be safe out in Iowa or Denver or Washington, D.C.; who smiled with joy when I told her I was writing a book and cried with joy when she read the manuscript. To my mother, to whom I could never say thank you enough, thank you for everything.

BIBLIOGRAPHY

The majority of information contained in this book was gathered from personal journal entries, photos, emails and memories from my experiences during the presidential campaigns; however, other sources were consulted to corroborate these experiences. Listed below are sources used in this research and verification of facts.

BOOKS

Alter, Jonathan. *The Center Holds: Obama and His Enemies*. New York: Simon & Schuster, 2013. Print.

Change We Can Believe In: Barack Obama's Plan to Renew America's Promise. New York: Three Rivers Press, 2008. Print.

Crotty, William and John S. Jackson III. *Presidential Primaries and Nominations*. Washington, D.C.: CQ Press, 1985. Print

Theis, Paul A. and William P. Stoponkus. *All About Politics: Questions and Answers on the U. S. Political Process*. New York: Bowker, 1972. Print.

PERIODICALS

Beaumont, Thomas. "New Iowa Poll: Obama Widens Lead Over Clinton." *Des Moines Register*, Jan. 1, 2008. Web. 13 Aug. 2009.

Davis, Robert AND James Strong. "Chicago Mourns Mayor Washington, Council Picks New Mayor Next Week." *Chicago Tribune*, Nov. 27, 1987. Web. 13 Aug. 2009.

Flannery, Mike. "Obama Campaign Headquarters Buzzes With Excitement." *CBS 2 News*, Apr. 5, 2007. Web. 15 May 2009.

Graham, Nicholas. "Obama Family Secret Service Code Names." *Huffington Post*, Dec. 11, 2008. Web. 1 Jun. 2010.

Lynch, James Q. "What Happens at a Caucus?" *The Gazette*, November 17, 2007. Web. 10 Aug. 2009.

Schonfeld, Erick. "After Facebook And The Obama Campaign, Chris Hughes Takes a Post At General Catalyst." *TechCrunch*, March 17, 2009. Web. 15 May 2009.

Sweet, Lynn. "Obama's New HQ Has Room to Move." *Chicago Sun-Times*, April 6, 2007. Web. 15 May 2009. 15 Aug. 2009.

SPEECHES

"Barack Obama's Speech at the Democratic National Convention." *New York Times*, August 28, 2008. Web. 1 Sept. 2010.

"Barack Obama's Speech On Race." *New York Times*, Mar. 18, 2008. Web. 15 Aug. 2009.

"Bill Clinton's Convention Speech." *New York Times*, Aug. 27, 2008. Web. 29 Jul. 2010.

"Joseph R. Biden's Convention Speech." *New York Times*, Aug. 27, 2008. Web. 29 Jul. 2010.

Phillips, Macon. "President Barack Obama's Inaugural Address." *The White House Blog. The White House*. Jan. 21, 2009. Web. 15 Aug. 2009.

"Sarah Palin – Speech at the Republican National Convention." *New York Times*, Sept. 3, 2008. Web. 1 Sept. 2010.

VIDEOS

OFA Grassroots Finance Committee. "Michelle Carnes Shares Her Experience as a Member of the Grassroots Finance Committee." Online video clip. *YouTube*. You Tube, 16 Aug. 2008. Web. 1 Sept. 2010.

INDEX

About the Publisher

Let us bring your story to life! With Life to Legacy, we offer the following publishing services: manuscript development, editing, transcription services, ghostwriting, cover design, copyright services, ISBN assignment, worldwide distribution, and eBooks.

Throughout the entire production process, you maintain control over your project. We are here to serve you. Even if you have no manuscript at all, we can ghostwrite your story for you from audio recordings or legible handwritten documents.

We also specialize in family history books, so you can leave a written legacy for your children, grandchildren, and others. You put your story in our hands, and we'll bring it to literary life! We have several publishing packages to meet all your publishing needs.

Call us at: 877-267-7477, or you can also send e-mail to: Life2Legacybooks@att.net. Please visit our Web site:

www.Life2Legacy.com

www.ingramcontent.com/pod-product-compliance
Lightning Source LLC
Chambersburg PA
CBHW060744100426
42813CB00032B/3396/J